NEGOTIATION + INFLUENCE = SUCCESS

Quick Lessons to Help You Win in Corporate Life

BY GIUSEPPE CONTI

PASSIONPRENEUR® PUBLISHING

Negotiation + Influence = Success
Copyright © 2025 By Giuseppe Conti
First published in 2025

Print: 978-1-76124-233-5
E-book: 978-1-76124-234-2
Hardback: 978-1-76124-235-9

Publishing information
Publishing and design facilitated by Passionpreneur Publishing
A division of Passionpreneur Organization Pty Ltd
ABN: 48640637529

Melbourne, VIC | Australia
www.passionpreneurpublishing.com

TABLE OF CONTENTS

Testimonials ix

INTRODUCTION 1

Chapter 1
NEGOTIATING AND INFLUENCING IN MY
      PROFESSIONAL LIFE 5

CHAPTER 2
A NEW PERSPECTIVE ON NEGOTIATION
      AND INFLUENCING 19
Let's clarify the terms 20
Misconceptions about negotiation and influencing 21
8 principles for negotiation mastery 23
8 steps to influence an internal stakeholder 26
An overview of the content 29

Chapter 3
NEGOTIATION AND INFLUENCING FUNDAMENTALS 33
3.1 Understanding the interests and priorities of
your counterparts 33
3.2 Ensuring the satisfaction of your counterpart 35
3.3 Adapting your approach in negotiation 37
3.4 Balance of power in negotiation 39
3.5 How to deal with emotions when negotiating 41
3.6 How to make a good first impression 44

3.7 Building rapport 46

3.8 Being trustworthy 48

3.9 Preparing for a negotiation 50

3.10 Chapter 3 in a nutshell 52

Chapter 4
CREATING VALUE IN NEGOTIATION 55

4.1 Gathering information during a negotiation 55

4.2 Exploiting differences in negotiation 57

4.3 Contingency agreements 59

4.4 Enhancing your questioning ability 61

4.5 How good are your listening skills? 63

4.6 Active listening – paraphrasing 65

4.7 Applying empathic listening 67

4.8 Chapter 4 in a nutshell 68

Chapter 5
CLAIMING VALUE IN NEGOTIATION 69

5.1 Making the first offer in a negotiation 69

5.2 Effective techniques in concession-making 73

5.3 Strengthening our power in negotiation 75

5.4 Negotiating styles and conflict management 77

5.5 Dealing with deadlocks in business negotiations 80

5.6 Negotiation tactics with no negative impact
on relationship 82

5.7 Using the limited authority tactic 84

5.8 Chapter 5 in a nutshell 85

Chapter 6
VIRTUAL NEGOTIATIONS 87

6.1 Negotiating over email 87

6.2 Telephone negotiations 89

6.3 Dealing with virtual negotiation challenges 91

6.4 Choosing the right communication tools for
virtual negotiations 93

6.5 Chapter 6 in a nutshell 95

Chapter 7
PROCUREMENT AND SALES NEGOTIATIONS 97

7.1 Fighting a price increase 97

7.2 How to 'condition' a supplier 99

7.3 Negotiating with Procurement 100

7.4 Typical negotiation mistakes in Procurement 102

7.5 Chapter 7 in a nutshell 104

Chapter 8
BROADENING YOUR NEGOTIATION SKILLS 107

8.1 Defining the negotiation process 107

8.2 Team negotiations 109

8.3 Preparing for cross-cultural negotiations 112

8.4 Managing cross-cultural team negotiations 115

8.5 Nonverbal communication 117

8.6 Dealing with internal negotiations 119

8.7 Ethics and negotiation 121

8.8 Creativity in negotiation 124

8.9 Negotiating with family and friends..........................126

8.10 Ensuring a response to your questions in
a negotiation...130

8.11 How to get out of a deadlock.................................132

8.12 Chapter 8 in a nutshell...134

Chapter 9
ADVANCED NEGOTIATION..139

9.1 Preventing people from lying to you 139

9.2 Negotiating a long-term agreement.........................141

9.3 Multiparty negotiations...143

9.4 Managing internal and external negotiations..................145

9.5 Multiple Equivalent Simultaneous Offers (MESOs) 147

9.6 Emotional intelligence and negotiation...................150

9.7 How Large Language Models are
revolutionising negotiation...152

9.8 Chapter 9 in a nutshell...155

Chapter 10
CAREER MATTERS 159

10.1 How to get a raise – knowing your worth 159

10.2 How to get a raise – making the request...............162

10.3 How to get a raise – dealing with a negative reply 164

10.4 Office politics – networking 166

10.5 Office politics – unwritten rules...............................168

10.6 Chapter 10 in a nutshell..170

Chapter 11

INFLUENCING TECHNIQUES.. 171

11.1 The persuasive power of framing 171

11.2 Applying the priming effect 175

11.3 Leveraging social pressure..177

11.4 The winner's curse..179

11.5 Overconfidence 181

11.6 Dealing with confirmation bias.......................................183

11.7 Flattery and compliments... 186

11.8 Chapter 11 in a nutshell...188

Chapter 12

BROADENING YOUR INFLUENCING SKILLS 191

12.1 Influencing others using logic or emotion............................191

12.2 Building coalitions 193

12.3 Offering the right incentives to motivate...........................195

12.4 How to recognise a real expert.......................................197

12.5 Gender differences in influencing at
business meetings...199

12.6 How to break good or bad news to your boss................202

12.7 How your voice strengthens the credibility of
your message..204

12.8 Chapter 12 in a nutshell 206

Conclusion...209

Author Bio.. 213

Extras: If You Enjoyed This Book..215

Acknowledgements...217

Works Cited..221

TESTIMONIALS

Owen Darbishire (Negotiation Professor, University of Oxford): 'Giuseppe Conti has a justified reputation as an outstanding communicator of the skills that everyone can learn to become truly effective at negotiation and influence. This book gets to the heart of building precisely the tools that are essential to master, in a form that is both incredibly practical and digestible. What also makes this book particularly valuable is that it will help people apply negotiation and influence skills to manage their own careers much more successfully.'

David Galan (Head of Procurement, Nestlé Health Science): As a professional navigating the complexities of corporate environments, I have found Giuseppe Conti's insights to be invaluable. This book distils over 25 years of experience into practical strategies that are not only easy to understand but also immediately applicable in real-world scenarios. Giuseppe's ability to simplify complex concepts is remarkable. His emphasis on the importance of relationships and the subtle dynamics of influence resonates deeply, reminding us that success is often built outside the formal meeting room.'

Alessandro de Luca (Chief Information Officer, Merck): 'Having known Giuseppe Conti for over three decades—as a colleague, a friend, and a sharp strategic thinker—I can confidently say this book is a reflection of the clarity, depth, and real-world insight that he brings to every conversation.

Negotiation + Influence = Success is not just another business book; it's a hands-on manual filled with practical wisdom that only years of experience can offer. Whether you're navigating high-stake deals or seeking to build influence in complex corporate environments, this book is a must-read.'

Luigi Staccoli (Chief Procurement Officer, MSC Cargo): 'After nearly 25 years of managing complex negotiations across different cultures—and navigating both internal conflicts within organizations and external challenges with suppliers and partners—I've learned that there's always room to grow and refine one's approach. Negotiation is a daily part of life, whether you're a seasoned professional or simply managing everyday interactions. Giuseppe Conti has helped my team and me take our skills to the next level through his insightful training, coaching, and structured method-ology. The result? A high-performing procurement function delivering outstanding results. This book distils those same principles—making it an essential read for anyone looking to negotiate more effectively, in any setting.'

Nicolas Passaquin (Chief Procurement Officer, Telia, author of *Procurement & The Book: How to Master Procurement*): 'As a Chief Procurement Officer and negotiation coach who has participated in Giuseppe's workshops, I have witnessed firsthand the immense value he brings through his highly professional and practical approach. His book encapsulates the same world-class strategies and insights that have made him a top-ranked negotiation guru, making it an indispens-able resource for anyone looking to excel in negotiation.'

Stéphane Rosenberg (Head of Procurement, International Olympic Committee): 'Giuseppe's in-depth expertise in negotiations, combined with his remarkable ability to teach and convey complex concepts, has greatly benefited our teams. He is definitely a go-to expert for organizations looking to enhance their negotiation strategies and capabilities. While nothing can quite replace the experience of working with Giuseppe in person, I am delighted that his book encapsulates years of extensive business experience, offering practical and actionable insights.'

Suzanne de Janasz (Negotiation Professor, London Business School, author of *Negotiation and Dispute Resolution*): 'In this broad, down-to-earth collection of negotiation concepts, examples, and advice, Giuseppe Conti breaks down the contextual and procedural components of negotiating and offers practical advice for handling all kinds of negotiations. His work reflects the important way that teaching and practice inform each other. Conti shares important negotiation knowledge and lessons from his decades of experience working in procurement and sales at blue-chip companies... polished by years of experience teaching MBAs and executives around the world.'

Hind Beaujon (Chief Sales Officer, Pfeiffer Vacuum): 'In complex industrial negotiations, success is rarely the result of improvisation. It requires structure, rigorous preparation, and a shared language to align internal and external stakeholders. Through our collaboration—both at Business School Lausanne and with my team—Giuseppe brought a disciplined, strategic approach that elevated how we prepare, align, and execute in high-stakes negotiations. His method shifted our mindset from reactive to proactive, placing value creation and internal alignment at the core of our negotiation process. The impact was immediate and measurable. In his book *Negotiation + Influence = Success: Quick Lessons to Help You Win in Corporate Life*, we find the quality and clarity that Giuseppe consistently brings to his work. As a sharp negotiator and thoughtful educator, he has a rare ability to turn complex dynamics into practical, actionable tools. I'm confident this book will become a valuable reference for professionals seeking to drive strategic value through negotiation and influence.'

Fred Perreand (VP Global Supply Chain Operations, Emerson): 'I have worked with Giuseppe for almost a decade. He provides a combination of practical case studies based on a theoretical framework to improve negotiation skills. Participants will be engaged by Giuseppe's light and humorous style. They will leave more confident and empowered to deliver a step change in results.'

Stéphane Lury (CEO, Hagerty): 'I've known Giuseppe for 25+ years—half of my life. He is one of those people you meet at work (during our early P&G years in the 1990s), knowing from the start that you will build a long-term relationship with them. The first quality I love about Giuseppe, and the one which probably made the difference when choosing who will be the No. 1 negotiation guru in the world, is his deeply empathic personal style. Giuseppe will always ask how you are, along with all the related questions to ensure he doesn't overlook any aspect of your personal and professional life.

The second quality is his strong professionalism and deep expertise, first as a procurement executive for multinationals and now as a 'dottore' transmitting his decades of learning to others. Having attended several workshops led by Giuseppe, I have always learnt something concrete that I have been able to reapply in my professional and personal life. This book is a 'condensé' of all those workshops and expertise that can be useful at all levels of negotiation, from beginners learning the basics to those seeking more advanced insights. I am sure this book will become a well-deserved international success.'

Jan Hansen (Chief Procurement Officer, Novartis): 'I had the opportunity to learn from Professor Giuseppe Conti through several negotiation and influencing workshops over the past years. These sessions have been an incredibly valuable learning experience. His insights significantly strengthened our approach and helped participants build confidence in real-world negotiation scenarios. Through practical exercises and examples, Professor Conti created an engaging environment for developing and refining skills. This book brings his expertise to a broader audience and will be a valuable resource for procurement professionals looking to enhance their capabilities.'

To my three daughters, Emma, Sara, and Luisa,
the biggest joy of my life.

INTRODUCTION

The news arrived in the middle of the night. I was at a retreat in Phuket, Thailand to write this book. **I was ranked #1 among the Top 30 Global Gurus for Negotiation**, the only ranking available in the world of negotiation, a sort of Oscar® in our field.

Was this a dream or reality?

Yes, it seemed to be true, although this ranking clearly exceeded my skills in and contribution to the world of negotiation. Indeed, I had taught at all the top 10 business schools in Europe, creating videos, podcasts, webinars, and live events, as well as writing articles, but had not yet written a book to share my ideas with the world. This recognition clearly gave me the motivation to make an extra effort to put my thoughts on paper and share with you what I have learnt during my career.

One of the landmarks of my success as a professor, trainer and lecturer has been my ability to communicate complex ideas in a simple way, with real-life examples. There is a quote by Steve Jobs—'Simple can be harder than complex: You have to work hard to get your thinking clean to make it simple.'—which has inspired my work for this book. I decided to make a book of 68 short segments aiming to offer the reader practical tips and fresh perspectives. The complex has been made simple.

As the message has been simplified, sometimes you may feel that you know it all already. That's OK, because these ideas may work for someone else. Sometimes, you may notice a small change that you could implement in the way you negotiate and influence. Those small changes can make a huge difference in your results, just like certain techniques can make a small difference in speed when running in a race, and this small difference can enable you to win the gold medal.

Make sure to highlight those key points that will enhance your skills, then convert them into concrete actions. Also, look for tools or suggestions you can share with other people at work or home. I aimed to make the content of this book as concrete as possible, so you can apply it for yourself and teach it to others. This is your opportunity to start changing your career path and your life by obtaining superior results while enjoying better relationships with the people around you.

The aim of this book is not to provide a comprehensive theoretical basis about the world of negotiation and influencing, because there are already plenty of great resources out there.

Instead, I'd like to share several small, practical methods I learned during my 25+ years negotiating in a corporate environment. Further learning opportunities came while interacting with bright workshop participants at top global business schools, at Fortune 500 companies, and across several contexts.

Because of my decision to include many short paragraphs, this book suits those seeking practical techniques to use in their daily life. You can read this on the go, while at work, or even at bedtime. The tips are easy to grasp and relatable. At the end of each chapter, you will find an overview of the key ideas we covered in the different paragraphs.

Most importantly, I hope this book will inspire you to take action by changing some of your behaviours. In fact, although the study of negotiation and influence is a science, the practice is an art. Start making changes in the way you interact with people, noticing what works and what does not. I hope you will take a minute to let me know how you put the learning from this book into practice.

So, let's get started. In the next chapter, you will discover some of the negotiation and influencing challenges I have experienced in my own life.

CHAPTER 1

NEGOTIATING AND INFLUENCING IN MY PROFESSIONAL LIFE

What prompted me to teach at the top 10 business schools in Europe?

I grew up in Calabria, in the South of Italy, the country's poorest region. Negotiation—or, more accurately, bargaining—has been part of my life since I was a kid. Opportunities for negotiation and influencing were frequent, whether shopping at the market or dealing with my three wonderful elder sisters.

My professional career as a negotiator started in February 1994. I was already working at Procter & Gamble (P&G) and was promoted from Process Engineer in a manufacturing plant to Purchasing Manager in P&G's European Headquarters in Brussels. I was responsible for P&G's purchases of resins and masterbatches that were used mainly to produce P&G plastic bottles for detergents. It was a total spend of $US300 million across Europe, Africa and the Middle East—quite an exciting challenge for a recent Engineering graduate student.

The excitement of the new job and the joy of meeting my future wife in Brussels were mitigated by some big challenges at work. The market for resins, such as high-density polyethylene or polypropylene, is extremely volatile and I had just taken on this new responsibility at the wrong time. **Market prices started to skyrocket** and, since the whole market operated on monthly price negotiations, we had no price protection from existing contracts. Our prices to customers were pretty much fixed for the year, while our costs were set to sharply increase. To make things worse, my predecessor had not forecast this price increase; it therefore came as a big surprise to management, negatively impacting all our estimates. In the meantime, my predecessor had left the company. The pressure was on me to keep prices down!

While on the waiting list to attend a negotiation workshop, I had to manage the crisis on my own. Lacking much expertise in this area, my newly promoted boss was putting additional pressure on me without providing much support. I wish I had read a negotiation book at that stage, like you are currently doing; unfortunately, I had not even thought about it. The only resources I could exploit at the time were the hard bargaining skills I had learnt during my adolescence. I started becoming involved in frequent and difficult monthly price negotiations with my suppliers, triggering endless heated arguments. Of course, P&G was a big buyer, but my suppliers were equally large petrochemical companies such as TotalEnergies, Dow Chemicals and BP. With my bargaining skills, I managed to postpone and mitigate the price increase. Still, prices went up and we faced a negative variance vs the initial forecast.

I realised that I had to strengthen my negotiation skills. I attended my first negotiation training, eagerly read a couple of negotiation books, listened to 12 audio cassettes on the topic and **started to reflect on and learn from my own experience**. Although at the time a lot of focus was on the price, as the Procurement team was measured on cost savings and cost avoidances, I learnt that negotiation was more than bargaining. If I wanted to obtain a better price, I could bring other variables to the negotiation table that would sweeten the deal for my counterpart. In addition, approaching negotiation with a learning attitude was more powerful than approaching it as a battle of arguments. Emotions and psychology were now part of the equation, contributing to better outcomes. I also started to take a more strategic approach to negotiation and influencing our suppliers. I was so committed and driven to be successful that I ended up working very hard, staying in the office until midnight two or three times each week. I really wanted to make a change and have an impact.

My commitment, hard work and strategic approach to negotiation and influencing was starting to pay off. Even though the resins market was operating based on monthly price negotiations, I was able to establish long-term agreements with our strategic suppliers, giving us a huge advantage over the market price. Results were well above target. I thought the timing was right to meet the Purchasing Director, three levels above me, and **ask for a promotion from Manager to Senior Manager**.

I still remember my galloping heart rate as I was getting ready to knock on the Director's door. He was extremely smart, big and intimidating with a deep voice, as well as an amazing negotiator. In fact he was my first role model for negotiation. I entered the door and made my request: to be promoted to Senior Manager. He quickly replied: 'How can I give you a promotion, Giuseppe? I do not hear much about what you are doing.' It was indeed true that I was purely focusing on maximising the results for P&G, without bothering to write nice reports or make beautiful presentations. In addition, since the P&G HQ was full, my department was in a separate building a few hundred metres away. Although this was not very far away, it was far enough to prevent senior management from visiting us often. Consequently, the Purchasing Director did not even know how hard I was consistently working for the success of the company.

When confronted with this objection, I tried to challenge him and said: 'How about my new strategic approach with suppliers, which is delivering great results and giving P&G a competitive advantage?'. He retorted: 'The new strategy was developed by John!'. John (not his real name) was my direct boss. I had focused purely on performance without working on my image, receiving little exposure due to the remote physical location and not having much luck with my boss. Unsurprisingly, I did not get the promotion!

As I analysed this matter with my mentor Alessandro, now a C-level executive at a leading multinational company, I learnt an important lesson about career negotiations. He explained to me that success in companies comes from multiple factors, later referred as the **PIE Model**:

- 30% **Performance** (contributions, full utilization of skills and abilities, impact on business results)
- 30% **Image** (reputation, credibility, perception, style)
- 30% **Exposure** (visibility to executive leadership, visibility to broad networks, crucial roles, sponsorship)
- 10% **Luck**.

For more insights on the PIE Model, you may want to check out *Empowering Yourself* by Harvey Coleman,[1] which expresses very similar concepts (although with different percentages).

To stay on the topic of **career management**, let me share another personal story from a few years later. I was headhunted out of P&G to join Novartis in Switzerland to help build the Strategic Procurement organisation in the company. P&G was seen as a pioneer in the world of Procurement. In fact, in the 90s I was already negotiating global agreements across Business Units, while most of the industry was operating on a local basis. As a result, P&G talents were in demand in the recruiting market and several of my former colleagues became C-level executives. I was lucky to be surrounded by so many bright minds during my nine years at P&G, with several of them still my friends.

Having now moved to a new country and a new company, I also had to understand a new company culture. At Novartis, there was a tradition of the senior executives going to the Fisherman's Pub for a drink on Friday afternoons. Several of the senior executives were British at the time, and they brought the tradition of drinking at the pub to Switzerland. I am not a big drinker, and had three lovely daughters at home waiting for me. When I had to make the choice on what to do on Friday at the end of my workday, my decision was clearly to go home and spend time with my family. As a result, I would go to the pub only once or twice per year.

Now, imagine that a couple of years later, you are a member of senior management who had to make a decision

---

1   H.J.J. Coleman, *Empowering Yourself: The Organizational Game Revealed*, 2nd ed. (AuthorHouse, 2010).

on a promotion between two equally qualified candidates. One is Giuseppe (me), whom you only meet from time to time in formal meetings. The other is Bill, whom you meet every Friday at the pub. Your family knows Bill's, and you both support the same football team. In this scenario, who is more likely to get the promotion?

This reminds us that **our influence within an organisation is not limited to formal meetings**. Many decisions are made at the pub, just as many relationships are formed when travelling with colleagues or celebrating at the quarterly Sales meetings.

Having learned this lesson, I was eager to pursue opportunities to increase my influence outside the meeting room. A few years later, I accepted a new job as Procurement Director at Firmenich (now DSM-Firmenich), in Switzerland's Geneva area. After a couple of months with the company, my employer organised a 'Community Day', an event which gave employees the opportunity to assist some of the charitable associations in the region. As the topic was close to my heart, I decided to volunteer.

At the end of the Community Day, the company organised a cocktail gathering to thank those who had volunteered. While I was there, the CEO attended to personally thank his employees. As he walked around, he made sure to spend time with the new employees he had not yet met, so he stopped by to get to know me. He asked me about my first impressions of the company and I shared a number of positive elements, in particular the personal attention to employees that I had experienced during the onboarding phase. I then mentioned that having worked with two larger multinationals before, P&G and Novartis, I had noticed a number of things that were done differently at Firmenich, and that we could probably improve our operational efficiency by applying some of the other multinationals' ideas. I also mentioned that as a new employee, you often discover several things that could be changed, but after a while your environment becomes the new normal. It would therefore be good to collect ideas from the newcomers so we could come up with potential improvements. When he asked me for an example of what could be improved, I told him that the people from the 2nd level Helpdesk could access employees' computers without authorisation; this looked like a dangerous practice to me. Thanking me for the idea, he moved on to talk to other people.

When I arrived at the office the following morning, I already had a message on my voicemail from a member of the Executive Board. It said: 'I talked with Patrick (the CEO), and he mentioned to me your idea of collecting ideas from newcomers in order to improve the operational efficiency of the company. I wanted to let you know that I will be your executive sponsor for this project. Please call me back and let's get started!'.

As you can see, one informal chat at a cocktail event enabled me to establish a relationship with the CEO, work on a project with an Executive Board member, and progress one of the ideas that was close to my heart.

Another typical challenge in organisations is trying to **influence internal stakeholders** to buy into one of your projects or ideas. The challenge is even bigger when you are trying to influence someone two or three levels above you in the hierarchy. This was one of the challenges that was given to me by the Global Head of Procurement of Firmenich during my first months on the job. I had to get the Head of the largest Business Unit to start collaborating with Procurement.

At the time, Procurement did not have a great reputation in the company. (The Business Unit would rather have managed their purchases on their own than work with Procurement.) In order to change the situation, I set up a meeting with the Head of the Business Unit. My objective was to influence him to change the current practices and make sure that we put in place a regular collaboration between his Business Unit and Procurement.

The meeting looked challenging. I was a Director; he was an Executive Vice-President. I had just joined the company and had little network; he had been around for over 15 years and was very much appreciated by everyone. I was working in what was perceived as a 'support function', while he was leading the largest Business Unit at the core of the entire Firmenich business.

As I prepared for this meeting, I thought it was key to begin changing his perception of Procurement as a slow and bureaucratic function. I therefore wanted to convey to him a 'can-do' attitude and express my willingness to deliver value for him. While I knew it would not be easy, I thought I had a fair chance of success.

I went to meet the Head of the Business Unit in his own office. After being kept waiting for a while by his secretary, I entered his office. He was sitting on a big chair, while I was on a normal-sized one. We briefly introduced each other and started our discussion. Whenever some information was missing or needed some external perspective, I volunteered to provide it, conveying the 'can-do' attitude I had prepared for.

At the end of the meeting, all the required actions were for *me* to complete. With the Head of the Business Unit raising the bar after I had delivered my initial actions, we never began discussing concrete initiatives. We did a couple of projects together in the end, but nowhere near the regular collaboration I had envisaged as the meeting's ideal outcome.

As I reflected on this experience and as I continued to manage senior stakeholders for another 13 years of my corporate career, I distilled a few ideas on what I learned to do when aiming to establish '**peer-to-peer relationships**' with senior executives:

a) As part of the preparation, **make sure to profile your counterpart**. This means doing some research, mainly through your network, in order to learn about their interests, personality, communication preferences, and hobbies.

b) **Avoid being too deferential** (otherwise they perceive you as an inferior, not as a peer). This is a matter of language and posture. In some more hierarchical cultures, you are expected to show respect to more senior executives without positioning yourself as inferior.

c) **Encourage a detailed personal introduction**, most likely by being the first one to introduce yourself. Take this opportunity to highlight some common interests you discovered during the profiling phase.

d) At the first meeting, **do not present slides or bring anyone else**. Given you want to build the relationship, it is easier to build trust on a one-to-one basis. In addition, without slides, you can focus on building rapport with your audience rather than making them look at a screen.

e) As an outcome of the first meeting, **make sure there are actions for both sides to take**. Asking the senior executive to perform even a simple action has two benefits: It gives you the opportunity to provide positive feedback, as well as laying the foundations for requesting incremental commitments and completing some bigger tasks together.

f) For subsequent meetings, try to **meet in a neutral place** (like the company cafeteria) if you are co-located. By doing this, you will create a more equal dynamic.

g) **Retain your relationship with the top person**. If they suggest appointing someone else in their team, reply that you will also appoint someone in your team for the more operational discussions. Then, recommend having some form of regular discussion with the senior executive. If they insist on fully delegating this instead, it means that they were not persuaded about your added value!

So far, I have shared some stories from my corporate life; there are many others in the book. Still, while reading my bio, maybe you were intrigued by the fact that I am the only person in the field of negotiation who has **taught at each of the top 10 European business schools**. So, why was I invited to teach at such wonderful institutions as INSEAD, Oxford, IMD and HEC Paris?

I guess the starting point of my teaching expertise was in the genes: My father and mother were both teachers, as were two of my sisters. (My other sister was a fashion designer, but she also taught fashion.) I guess I also had to get into the teaching space!

This career path started at P&G, when I had the opportunity to become an internal trainer. The company asked people with a specific talent in an area to become trainers on top of their normal job. Being offered a 'Train the Trainer' workshop started my career as a trainer – just a small part of my daily job.

I stopped training others when I moved to Novartis, since the company used external trainers. That is, until the moment my friend Xavier informed me that the University of Geneva was looking for someone to teach Negotiation at a Master's Procurement program, and the school preferred someone with Procurement experience. So, I applied for the job and got it! After my first workshop at the University of Geneva in 2005 was very well received, they asked me to start teaching Change Management on the strength of my influencing expertise. My teaching career was starting to take shape.

The growth of my teaching activity from one business school to 19 across three continents, including each of the top 10 business schools in Europe, was simply a combination of delivering high-quality content and effective networking. For instance, the year after I met the husband of one of the IMD Directors, his wife came to watch my workshop and liked it. Afterwards, she asked me to start teaching at IMD. While I was running my workshop there, one of the students mentioned the workshop to his wife, who was working at SDA Bocconi in Milan. On her recommendation, I then started teaching at SDA Bocconi. Two years later, someone at IMD recommended me to INSEAD, and someone at INSEAD recommended me to the London Business School. Teaching was playing an increasingly large role in my life.

At the same time, I continued my corporate path and managed a portfolio career for 13 years. Then, I left the corporate world in 2018 to become a professor. I started to focus more intensively on growing my training company, Conti Advanced Business Learning (www.cabl.ch). I was determined to live my dream by following my calling, because it feels so good to do a job that you love. I hope you will also be able to find the job you were made for.

To conclude this first chapter, you may be interested to know how I became **2025's number one Global Guru for Negotiation**. The criteria that the Global Guru organisation,[2] the only organisation that creates a ranking in the field of negotiation (a sort of Oscar® in our field), uses to make their decisions are as follows:

- Public opinion – 30%
- Originality of ideas – 30%
- Impact of original ideas – 10%
- Practicality of ideas – 10%
- Presentation style – 10%
- Number of publications and writings – 5%
- Guru factor 5%.

My strengths lie in three areas:

a) Practicality of ideas. My ideas are based on solid research supported with real-life examples from my own experience at the negotiation table and in conference rooms influencing internal stakeholders.
b) Presentation style. Since I love what I do, my energy and passion come across during my delivery.

---

2   *Global Gurus*. www.globalgurus.org (accessed April 3, 2025).

c) Public opinion. I am working hard to spread knowledge across the world. Besides teaching at multiple business schools, I run workshops for corporate customers, write daily LinkedIn posts and a monthly article on the topic, record a new video each month, and run several webinars and live events. In the course of teaching in four continents each year, I build relationships of trust with many people around the world.

This book is the next step in my resolution to leave a legacy and help as many people as possible improve their ability to negotiate and influence. It can also help you identify how negotiation and influencing can be powerful accelerants to your career. Let's get started by looking at the structure of this book and how you can get the most out of it.

CHAPTER 2

A NEW PERSPECTIVE ON NEGOTIATION AND INFLUENCING

An enjoyable process

What comes to mind when you think about negotiation and influencing? What if we could turn these concepts into more enjoyable processes?

Our life is full of communication, and when we communicate, we also negotiate and influence. Look at your interactions, then count how many of these involve negotiations. We negotiate multiple times each day with colleagues, spouses, parents, bosses, shop owners, customers and service providers. Determining the deadline for a report, what movie to watch and the curfew for a party are all examples of negotiations and influencing activities in our daily lives.

Unfortunately, too often we look at negotiation and influencing as a difficult, complicated and competitive process. This is especially true for women, who (in an interesting US study) tended to see negotiation in similarly unpleasurable terms as 'going to the dentist'.[1]

---

1   L. Babcock and L. Laschever, *Women Don't Ask: Negotiation and the Gender Divide* (Princeton University Press, 2003).

One of the aims of this book is to help you change this perspective and become a better negotiator and influencer. Acquiring increased knowledge on this topic will help you become more self-confident and at ease with such conversations, making the process more enjoyable.

The great news is, good negotiators are more satisfied and less stressed at work.[2] A small difference in negotiating and influencing ability can make a huge impact on your results and overall career success. This is your opportunity to learn some key ideas to effectively manage both external and internal negotiations.

LET'S CLARIFY THE TERMS

The Cambridge Dictionary defines negotiation as 'the process of discussing something with someone in order to reach an agreement with them, or the discussions themselves.'[3]

Negotiation is a communication artform, as well as a way to dissolve conflicts and to enhance relationships. In many ways, it builds trust and authentic connections.

When talking about influence, I like to use this definition: 'Affecting the actions, behaviours, opinions or feelings of another person, without coercion.'

The reason many people tend to have a negative perspective on influence is that they may be confusing it with

2   K. Champika, "The Role of Negotiation Skills in Career Development and Organizational Effectiveness: A Study of Sri Lanka State Universities," *Science and Innovation* 3, no. 10 (October 2024): 190–4.

3   Cambridge Dictionary. (n.d.). Negotiation. In *Cambridge Online Dictionary*. Retrieved May 11, 2025, from https://dictionary.cambridge.org/dictionary/english/negotiation.

manipulation. Yet while the techniques used in both situations may be similar, the major difference is the *intent*. With influence, we are trying to get someone else to do something that is good for us, as well as being good for them or the company. With manipulation, however, we are trying to get someone to do something that is good for us but *not* good for them; in that case, the techniques and the intent are underhand, deceptive, and dishonest.

Let me also clarify the difference in this book between persuasion and influencing. We will look at persuasion as *a method where you present evidence, reasoning, and emotions to convince someone that a particular course of action is beneficial or correct*. It is an event, and it is a one-way approach.

In contrast, I see influencing as a medium- to long-term process of mutual influence. We build the right relationships, and the influencing process continues over time. A key message to retain is that influence is about *people*.

As the aim of this chapter is to give you a new perspective on negotiation and influencing, let's look at some common misconceptions about these concepts.

MISCONCEPTIONS ABOUT NEGOTIATION AND INFLUENCING

1. **Negotiation is all about compromise**: Many believe that negotiation means splitting things down the middle (perhaps 50/50 on each issue). In reality, effective negotiation often focuses on doing smart trades where you give up something of lower value to gain something of higher

value and on finding creative solutions that satisfy the interests of all parties, leading to win–win outcomes.

2. **The best negotiators are aggressive**: Some think that being tough and confrontational is the key to successful negotiation. However, practising collaboration, empathy, and active listening is the ideal way to achieve a superior outcome.

3. **Negotiation is only for sales or legal professionals or FBI agents**: This misconception limits the understanding of negotiation's relevance. In fact, negotiation skills are valuable in various contexts, from workplace discussions to personal relationships.

4. **You need to be a natural-born negotiator**: It is an often-repeated mantra that negotiation is an innate talent. In truth, negotiation is a skill that can be learned and improved through practice and education.

5. **You should always aim for the lowest price**: Many think that the goal of negotiation is to secure the lowest possible price. Instead, the focus should be on value—understanding what is truly important to both parties.

6. **Influencing is a one-time event**: Some see influencing as a single transaction. However, successful influencing often involves ongoing relationships and future interactions, making it essential to consider the long-term impact.

7. **Influencing is unethical**: This is often related to the confusion between influencing and manipulation. Rather than being exploitative, the approach to influencing we are recommending is based on strong relationships and long-term collaborations.

8. **You need to use tricks to influence**: Effective influence does not depend on tricks, threats,

deception or coercion, which are unlikely to be effective in the longer term as they will negatively impact your reputation. Instead, we will be using research-based persuasion principles that strengthen our ability to influence, without relying on deceptive techniques. Now that we have addressed some frequent misconceptions, let me share some positive practices, starting with negotiation and then moving into influencing.

8 PRINCIPLES FOR NEGOTIATION MASTERY

These 8 principles are derived from over 25 years of experience in the corporate world, analysing and reflecting on some of the typical mistakes we frequently tend to make at the negotiation table:

1. **Strengthen your BATNA well before the negotiation starts**. Effective negotiation is about preparation and anticipation. The BATNA (Best Alternative To a Negotiated Agreement), an acronym created by W. Ury and R. Fisher in their bestselling book *Getting to Yes*,[4] refers to a negotiator's best possible outcome if a negotiation fails. We should only close a negotiation if we reach a better outcome than our BATNA, which is our fallback or plan B. It is counterproductive to go into a negotiation with a weak BATNA, because you will feel obliged to

---

4   R. Fisher & W. Ury, *Getting to Yes: Negotiating Agreement Without Giving In* (Penguin Books, 1981).

close the deal with your counterpart. However, strengthening your BATNA in the corporate world usually takes a long time. We should therefore identify the difficult negotiations (where we are in a position of weakness) upfront, anticipate the challenge and change the dynamics well before the negotiation starts.

2. **Prepare the negotiation in writing**. All the negotiation literature agrees on the fundamental importance of preparation for effective negotiation, even calling preparation 90% of success. Unfortunately, I have often seen people neglect preparation in real-life situations. Because preparation is a proactive activity, not a compulsory requirement, it is easy to skip this fundamental step in our busy world. But I can assure you that if you prepare in writing, you will see a huge difference in your negotiation results. In our book website, which you can access via the below QR code, we included a simple negotiation preparation template for you to use.

3. **Build trust**. In the corporate world, long-term trust-based relationships are vital for the success of a company. While everyone understands the importance of trust, we may not always have clear ideas on what helps us to be perceived as trustworthy by our counterparts. See section 3.8 for more on this topic.

4. **Understand interests and priorities of the counterpart**. At the heart of effective negotiation is our ability to deeply understand what is important for our counterpart. This should happen in two phases: first in the preparation, when we spend time to estimate the other parties' interests and priorities; then during the negotiation, when we use questions, active listening, offering options, body-language reading and a number of other techniques to build a detailed understanding of what is really important to them.

5. **Approach negotiation with a learning attitude**. The approach that is applied more often at the negotiation table is to look at negotiation as a battle of arguments. This contributes to the idea of negotiation as a stressful and competitive process. I would instead recommend approaching negotiation, especially in the initial phase, with a learning attitude. Your aim should be to spend a substantial amount of time exchanging questions and actively listening.

6. **Think broader than price**. This is particularly a challenge for people in the Procurement area that are oriented towards cost savings and therefore tend to over-focus on price. As much as price is an important and a clearly measurable outcome of a negotiation, there are several other sources of value in the negotiation, either tangible (e.g. contract length, payment terms) or intangible (e.g. quality of the relationship, perceived fairness).

7. **Ensure it is good for them, great for us**. The win–win paradigm, made popular by the book *Getting to Yes* by W. Ury and R. Fisher, has been the dominant concept for over 20 years. The latest theory recommends that a

good negotiation should be able to both create and claim value, so that you can make it good for your counterpart and great for yourself.

8. **Make sure the counterpart leaves the negotiation satisfied.** Recognising that we will often end up negotiating with the same people in the corporate world, we should make sure that our counterpart leaves the negotiation satisfied even if we were able to secure a bigger share of the total value. Inexperienced negotiators may struggle with this idea because they assume that they have to give better terms to their counterpart. The good news is that the satisfaction of the other party is more linked to the process than the outcome. We can increase the satisfaction of our counterpart via a number of simple behaviours such as listening to them, treating them with respect, offering good explanations, and making them work for the concessions they gain.

8 STEPS TO INFLUENCE AN INTERNAL STAKEHOLDER

One of the big challenges in corporate life is influencing internal stakeholders. As I run workshops with a number of multinational companies, I consistently hear that influencing internal stakeholders is more difficult than negotiating with external parties.

How can we make the process of influencing internal stakeholders a more collaborative, enjoyable and effective one? Here is an 8-step process that builds on our vision of influencing as a long-term process where we build the right relationships and create a context of mutual influence.

1. **Profiling**: A good starting point to increase our influencing ability is to do some research about our counterpart to understand their motivations and needs, but also their personality, communication style and hobbies.
2. **Preparation**: Preparing for an internal meeting is even less common than preparing for an external one, even though proper preparation can make a huge difference on the outcome. At the very least, be clear on the meeting's objective and prepare a few good questions.
3. **Introduction**: My former boss used to say that 99% of the time, we do business with people that we like. Those relationships are built over time as we get to know the people we interact with. Whenever you are meeting a stakeholder for the first time, make sure to comprehensively introduce yourself, discussing not only your current job but also your background, family, and personal interests. Ideally, you will mention some of the commonalities with your counterpart that you identified during the initial profiling phase.
4. **Context**: This is probably the most difficult element to learn. It refers to our ability to adapt to the context, starting with the capacity to increase our sensory acuity and be fully present in the moment. This includes being able to monitor interaction dynamics (reading the room, body language, voice variations, openness, positive vs negative energy) and adapting our communication based on the situation. Eliminating all distractions is essential, particularly during a virtual meeting.

5. **Questioning**: As Stephen Covey[5] taught us over 35 years ago, seek first to understand, then to be understood. An effective meeting starts with asking questions and better understanding your counterpart, not with trying to push your own agenda.

6. **Listening**: A complementary skill to questioning is active listening. We will only be able to gain the most from our questioning if we are fully focused on our counterpart and able to understand what is said, their feelings, what is left unsaid and their unspoken values.

7. **Speaking**: Only once we feel that we have fully understood our counterpart will the ideal moment to convey our message arrive. It will now be easier to focus on what's in it for them and to talk their language. Great communicators will also be able to leverage emotions and to increase their effectiveness via storytelling.

8. **Conclusion**: If you have done your preparation, you are clear on what you wanted to get out of this meeting. Make sure that you agree on a few concrete next steps that are aligned with the goal of the meeting and that will foster medium- to long-term collaboration with your counterpart.

---

5   S. R. Covey, *The 7 Habits of Highly Effective People* (Free Press, 1989).

AN OVERVIEW OF THE CONTENT

In the chapters to come, we will cover varied topics that will enable you to use your negotiation and influencing skills to your advantage and build better relationships.

Although the book focuses on the workplace, each topic can be practically applied to either professional or personal life. Let's look at what you will find in each chapter.

- **Negotiation and Influencing Fundamentals.** Here you will discover a range of the crucial attitudes and behaviours that are important for both negotiation and influencing.
- **Creating Value in Negotiation.** In this chapter, we will explore what is required to be effective during collaborative negotiations.
- **Claiming Value in Negotiation.** Here we will uncover the competitive side of negotiation—the behaviours that will enable you to maximise your share of the pie.
- **Virtual Negotiations.** Learning to negotiate through online channels is imperative. We will explore some of the different means of virtual negotiations and how to maximise their effectiveness.
- **Procurement and Sales Negotiations.** This chapter is intended for those working in Procurement and Sales who are seeking some more detailed advice.
- **Broadening your Negotiation Skills.** After covering the basics, we will enlarge our horizons with some new perspectives on negotiation (e.g. defining the negotiation process, team negotiations).

- **Advanced Negotiation.** To conclude the section on negotiation, we will look at a few more advanced topics, such as multiparty negotiations and preventing people from lying to you.
- **Career Matters.** Career negotiations are an important challenge in the corporate world. Here, you'll learn some key insights into the right way to ask for a raise and how to manage office politics ethically.
- **Influencing Techniques.** We will start our influencing journey by studying some of the most well-known techniques, including framing and confirmation bias.
- **Broadening your Influencing Skills.** This last chapter offers an opportunity to enlarge our influencing toolbox as well as understanding how to use each different technique effectively.

Each chapter consists of several short paragraphs, with each paragraph covering one specific point. As a result, the paragraphs can be read independently. We kept each one very short to include only the essential information. If you want to go deeper into a topic, you can find additional resources—one article and one video for each paragraph—on our book's website, accessible via the QR code below.

As a result, you can choose to read the book from beginning to end or, depending on the challenges that you are facing, jump to a specific chapter or paragraph.

Because of the modularity and conciseness of the book, you can use it as bedtime reading or to get some new insights in a few minutes when taking a break or commuting.

It is now time to get started with some of the negotiation and influencing fundamentals!

CHAPTER 3

NEGOTIATION AND INFLUENCING FUNDAMENTALS

3.1 UNDERSTANDING THE INTERESTS AND PRIORITIES OF YOUR COUNTERPARTS

To be effective in negotiation, it is important to understand who we are dealing with. How can you reliably understand more about the interests and priorities of the other party during a negotiation?

Here are three tips that can help you to be more effective:

- **Ask open-ended questions**. The most effective open-ended questions are the ones that start with *How* and *What*. Of course, asking questions starting with *Why* is also effective. The problem with the *Why* questions, though, is that they often make the other person defensive. If you want to ask a *Why* question, formulate a similar question which starts with *How* or *What*. For instance: 'What's behind your request to have a three-year contract?'. More insights (based on AI-supported research) on this fascinating topic are included in a *Harvard Business*

Review article[1] co-written by Jordi Quoidbach, one of my colleagues at Conti Advanced Business Learning.

- **Signal collaboration by sharing some information**. If you want to create an environment where you talk about common interests and priorities, you may want to start by sharing a small amount of information. Those who begin by doing this are not disadvantaging themselves, provided they share information judiciously. During a negotiation, share small nuggets of information and then stop. Before sharing more, ask your counterpart to reciprocate.

- **Explore options**. A simple technique is to use a **'what if'** question. What if we change the minimum order quantities? What if we rearrange the logistics for our deliveries? By using 'what if', you understand more about what is more or less valuable to the other party without making a firm commitment.

Building an understanding about the interests and priorities of our counterpart is fundamental to being able to identify **smart trades**. If something has a high value for you and a low value for your counterpart (or vice versa), you can create value by suggesting a trade: If you give me X, then I will give you Y.

1   M. Di Stasi, J. Quoidbach, and A. Wood Brooks, "The Most Effective Negotiation Tactic, According to AI," *Harvard Business Review* (September 2024).

3.2 ENSURING THE SATISFACTION OF YOUR COUNTERPART

During a negotiation, how much do you care about the satisfaction of your counterpart?

Unfortunately, too often, we do not care enough about how the other party will feel at the end of the negotiation. In 2019, I conducted a survey with 109 senior Procurement professionals from different continents (68% male and 32% female). I asked them to rank 20 key behaviours of effective negotiators. In this survey, 'Ensuring the satisfaction of the other party' was clearly ranked last.

There are benefits in making sure that your counterpart is satisfied. In business, you deal with people over time; if the other party is satisfied, you can count on the fact that the implementation will be smooth and that you will get preferential support in case of issues. Another benefit is that with a satisfied counterpart, you can trade satisfaction today for reaping the benefits tomorrow. You can tell them, 'Listen, this time you got a very good deal, so next time you will have to help me.' One more benefit is that you will be able to build a reputation as a fair negotiator. As your counterparts talk positively about you, more people will want to work with you and you will have more alternatives. In negotiation terms, this means that over time you will strengthen your BATNA (Best Alternative To a Negotiated Agreement), which will increase your power.

Participants in my workshops are often concerned about this idea of counterpart satisfaction, because they believe that they will have to give away some of their value in the process.

Here are five suggestions to increase the satisfaction of the other party without giving your own value away:

- **Start high**. This gives you room for concessions, which your negotiation counterpart likes seeing you make.
- **Listen to them**. This is one of the simplest concessions that you can make.
- **Treat them fairly**. Show respect and understanding.
- **Give good explanations**. It is important to give a rationale whenever you are asking for something or making a concession.
- **Highlight your concession**. Explain to the other party that you are really making an effort in order to make a concession for them.

3.3 ADAPTING YOUR APPROACH IN NEGOTIATION

Should you adapt your approach in negotiation, or should you just stay consistent with your way of negotiating?

Let me share with you a couple of real-life examples that may give us the answer to this question.

In June of 1992, the infamous American company Enron engaged in negotiations with the government of India. They approached the negotiation with a view that time is money, so we have to move fast. However, they did not spend much time getting to know their counterparts and went directly into commercial discussions with the Indian company. As you may have guessed, they did not win the contract. Moreover, the Indian company made a public statement indicating that they decided not to work with the American company because they were not prepared to spend time building a relationship with them.

In another real-life situation, a Sales Director of a fast-moving consumer goods company in charge of sales for France was used to negotiating with retail companies like Carrefour and Auchan, known for their tough negotiation styles. He therefore responded with a similarly tough style. As his career evolved, he became the Marketing Director in a cosmetics company. Now he is working in partnership with marketing agencies, where his tough communication style is no longer appropriate.

As you have probably guessed from these two examples, it is necessary to adapt negotiation styles to suit the situation.

Here are five key elements that you may want to consider to adapt your negotiation style to different situations.

1. Know your own preferred negotiation style. Do you tend to be more compromising, competitive, collaborative, accommodating, or avoidant? **Knowing your default negotiation style is a good starting point**.

2. **How about the negotiation style of the person you are dealing with?** Especially if you are in a recurrent business relationship, you have probably already built a good understanding of the typical behaviour of the person you are negotiating with.

3. **Cultural differences**. Depending on their country of origin, company culture or other cultural elements, your counterpart may have certain preferences. You may then want to adapt your style. For instance, if you are going to negotiate in China, a country culture that values relationships, you are more likely to spend time in informal dinners and starting the meeting with small talk.

4. **The balance of power**. Are you in a stronger or weaker position? Who has the strongest BATNA (Best Alternative To a Negotiated Agreement); i.e. what would you do if you are not able to reach an agreement with your counterpart? Who has the most to lose if there is no deal?

5. Often used by Procurement people is the **analysis of the Kraljič matrix**. It is a method used to segment the purchases of a company developed in 1983 by Peter Kraljič[2] (with whom I had the pleasure to share the stage at ProcureCon Europe in 2015). If your forthcoming negotiation is linked to a 'bottleneck' category, where the seller has most of the power, your behaviour will differ from negotiating in a 'leverage' category, where the buyer has most of the power.

---

2   P. Kraljič, "Purchasing Must Become Supply Management," *Harvard Business Review* (September 1983).

3.4 BALANCE OF POWER IN NEGOTIATION

How do you understand who has more power in a negotiation?

There are a number of factors that influence our ability to wield power in a negotiation. Some of the most common ones are knowledge/information, preparation, willingness to take risks, a sense of urgency, the dependency between the two parts, and the skills of the negotiators.

If you are looking for a quick method to evaluate the power in a negotiation, I suggest asking yourself a couple of questions.

What are the BATNA strengths of the two parties? If you are unable to close a deal, the BATNA (Best Alternative To a Negotiated Agreement) is the path that you will follow. In addition, you will need to estimate the BATNA of the other party. You will then be in the position to understand what their relative strength is. The ability to walk away from the deal is a key source of power.

Another simple way to estimate the balance of power in negotiation is to ask yourself: '**Who has the most to lose, if we are not able to reach an agreement?**'.

Once you have evaluated those two elements, consider these two ideas to strengthen your power. One is to **change the situation—or at least the other party's** *perception* **of the situation, since what matters is the perceived power, so that you have less to lose and they have more**. A second idea is that **you have more power than you think**. Since we know all the limitations on our side, but not the limitations on the other side, we have a tendency to underestimate our power. Otherwise stated, when we do not have great alternatives (i.e. a weak BATNA), we assume we are in a weak position; but our counterpart may also lack great alternatives!

A final consideration regarding the tendency to overuse power when we are in a strong position. This is often causing resentment, a willingness to retaliate and broken relationships.

3.5 HOW TO DEAL WITH EMOTIONS WHEN NEGOTIATING

A few years ago, when my daughters were still young, my wife and I were looking for a new babysitter. The young woman was supposed to come to our home to be interviewed by us. I asked my wife to let me handle the discussion about the hourly rate. The babysitter arrived; she was very nice and friendly. After a while, we told her that we were interested in her starting work. Then she mentioned: 'I am really happy that I am able to get a job because, to be honest, my father has been unemployed for the past 18 months, and his unemployment benefits have dried up. I am looking forward to increasing my financial contribution to the family.' As you can imagine, after listening to her sad story, it was hard for me to start negotiating her hourly rate.

The first tip is therefore to learn to **use both rational and emotional messaging** in your negotiations. I usually do not use emotional messages during big negotiations when there are a number of people on both sides of the table. I prefer to use the emotional messages during the coffee break when discussing with my commercial counterpart: 'Barbara, we worked well during the last three years. It seems that the negotiation is at a deadlock stage. I need your support; can you please…'

Let's now take a different perspective on emotions. Should you express your emotions? Should you get upset, for instance, during a negotiation? **It is good to show your emotions** as long as you are able to control them. If you get carried away by your emotions, then this decreases your effectiveness in negotiations. If you are afraid, then you are unlikely to make good decisions. If you are angry, then you are unlikely to be able to listen effectively to the other party. So, whenever you feel that your emotions are overwhelming you, use a technique to control them. Taking a break is powerful way to do this, as our emotions tend to be transient and only last for a few minutes. For some, this may involve taking a deep breath, while others may want to count to ten or one hundred. You may also want to learn to recognise the body language associated with a change of your emotional state so that you get an early warning that your emotional state is changing. Choose what works for you—just make sure to **control your emotions during the negotiation**.

An interesting perspective on emotions in negotiation comes from a book by two Harvard Professors, Roger Fisher and Daniel Shapiro.[3] Rather than reacting to a multitude of changing emotions that occur during a negotiation, they recommend working on '**5 Core Concerns**' that are important to almost everyone in virtually every negotiation to enable us to build positive emotions and overcome negative ones. These five Core Concerns are:

- **Express appreciation**. Listen to your counterpart, find merit in what they say, then show it.
- **Respect autonomy**. Avoid 'take it or leave it' language and ultimatums.
- **Build affiliation**. Look for ways to connect, talk about shared problems.

3   R. Fisher and D. Shapiro, *Beyond Reason: Using Emotions as You Negotiate* (Penguin, 2005).

- **Acknowledge status**. Respect their experience as well as their expertise.
- **Enhance their role**. Ask for their advice, do a joint round of brainstorming.

I encourage you to read Fisher and Shapiro's great book if you are interested in more information on the topic.

3.6 HOW TO MAKE A GOOD FIRST IMPRESSION

Are you giving a strong first impression to people that you are meeting for the first time? Here are some tips that can help you in these important situations.

- **Quality of your written communication**: Even before people meet you, they are going to make up their mind about you, based on your documents and email exchanges. Think about how you can sharpen your written communication.
- **Nonverbal communication style**: If you want to convey a positive image nonverbally, adopt an open posture, keep a good level of eye contact, smile, and maybe lean forward slightly. Additionally, consider mirroring the gestures and posture of the person you're dealing with. Other nonverbal elements include standing tall with shoulders back, walking with confidence, keeping your chin angle down, avoiding front-on body display, keeping your palms up, and having a firm handshake.
- **Vocal variety**: To convey a positive image with your voice, you want a medium pitch (not too high, not too low). Then, ensure a good variation of your voice in terms of volume, speed and intonation. In addition, you may want to match the speed and volume of the person you are dealing with.
- **Take care of your appearance**: Choose clothes that fit well, appropriate make-up, jewellery (if appropriate), polished shoes, a nice watch, well-maintained hair, an overall look that fits with the context.

- **Establish your credibility while conveying a genuine interest in the other party**: We want to highlight our past experience and expertise that makes us a reliable counterpart. At the same time, we want to start with something relevant to them, so let them talk about their interests and priorities and show that we care.

How people perceive us comes down to two core components: **warmth** and **competence**. You should make sure to deliver strong first impressions on both elements by coming across as a nice person with whom the other person would enjoy working with and at the same time remaining credible and professional.

3.7 BUILDING RAPPORT

Imagine we are in 19th century Great Britain. At that time, there were two strong political figures, Disraeli and Gladstone. The two men were rivals, competing for 30 years to be Prime Minister. A journalist interviewed both of them, giving his feedback: 'I spoke with Gladstone and I felt he is one of the brightest persons in the country. Then, I spoke with Disraeli, and he made me feel that I was one of the brightest persons in the country.' Certainly, Disraeli had the ability to connect with people and make them feel at their best.

You can also be more effective in building rapport with other people. Let me share with you three simple pieces of advice that you may find useful.

The first one is to **look for similarities** because we are all connected to people who are like us. For instance, I remember when I was in charge of indirect Procurement at the global headquarters of a large multinational. My job involved dealing with many different stakeholders across different corporate functions (Marketing, R&D, IT, HR,...). As I was meeting a new stakeholder, I consistently encouraged a fairly long mutual personal introduction. Inevitably, we would discover some similarities. Maybe we went to the same school, or we worked in the past for the same company, or we both had three children. And as we found a commonality, this created the basis for a more effective relationship and interaction between the two of us.

A second piece of advice is to **make effective compliments**. I am not talking about flattery. Look for something that you really appreciate in the other person and say it with genuine emotion. To reinforce the compliment, justify your statement and then ask them a question on the topic, such as 'What do you do in order to apply this competence on a daily basis?'. Not only will this reinforce the compliment, it will also give you the opportunity to learn something more about this useful skill.

The third and last piece of advice is to use the **technique of mirroring**. When two people get along well, they naturally mirror each other. This shows up in similar posture, similar movements, and even similar voice volume and speed. The technique of mirroring encourages you to use body language to create this kind of harmony. When you meet someone, make sure to take a similar posture, make similar types of movements, and ensure you use a similar speed and volume of voice.

3.8 BEING TRUSTWORTHY

We all believe in the importance of trust in personal and business relationships. The challenge is that we may all have a different definition of trust. **Trust comes from a combination of being trustworthy and trusting the other party**.

How do you evaluate if a person is trustworthy? What are the key factors that people use to determine if you are a trustworthy person?

To give you an insight into trustworthiness, I want to share with you a framework that has proven to be effective since 2001, when it was first published in the book *The Trusted Advisor*.[4] This is called the Trust Equation and it is expressed as follows:

$$\text{Trustworthiness} = \frac{\text{Credibility} + \text{Reliability} + \text{Intimacy}}{\text{Self-Orientation}}$$

Let's understand the four components of the Trust Equation.

Credibility. In a business environment, credibility is associated with your competence. Does your counterpart know their job, the product, the market? When dealing with your internal stakeholders, do you convey the image that you know the business?

Reliability. This is about keeping your promises and walking the talk. If you tell your boss that you will send her the presentation by Friday, do you *really* send it by Friday?

---

4   D. H. Maister, C. H. Green, and R. M. Galford, *The Trusted Advisor* (Touchstone, 2001).

Intimacy. This element captures the emotional component of the relationship. Do you feel safe to share information or discuss a difficult topic with your counterpart?

Self-Orientation. You will be perceived as less trustworthy if you tend to focus only on your own interests and priorities rather than also paying attention to your counterpart's interests and priorities.

To be perceived as trustworthy, make sure to be competent and reliable, build good relationships with your counterpart and show that you care about the other party.

3.9 PREPARING FOR A NEGOTIATION

We have often heard that preparation is vital to achieve success in negotiations, or even that preparation comprises 90% of success.

So, how do we prepare for negotiation?

If you have gone through negotiation training, you have probably received a negotiation preparation template. If not, you will find a simple template on the website for this book.

If you do not have access to a good template, let me share a simple way to prepare for negotiation.

It starts with the idea of understanding your counterpart (see 3.1). To be a better negotiator, you want to look at the deal from both sides (assuming that there are only two parties involved).

Your preparation will therefore involve going through these key topics for both sides:

- **Interests**: What are my interests? What is really important to me in this negotiation? What are their interests?
- **Arguments**: What arguments will I use to support my views? Can I use objective criteria to make my arguments stronger (e.g. by making reference to publicly available information)? What arguments are they likely to use (and how can I reply to them)?
- **Questions**: What questions do I want to ask? What key piece of information am I missing?
- **Answers**: What questions are they likely to ask and what is likely to be my reply?
- **Alternatives**: What am I going to do if I am not able to close a deal with this counterpart? What will be my best

alternative/BATNA? What are they likely to do if they do not close a deal with us? What is likely to be their best alternative/BATNA?

- **Initial requests**: What will my initial request be? What is their initial request likely to be?
- **Good results**: What is a good result for me? What is likely to be a good result for them?
- **Reservation prices**: What is my reservation price (my indifference point between a deal and no deal)? What is the limit for me? What do I estimate to be their reservation price?

By answering these questions for both parties, you have a simple methodology to prepare for negotiation. Filling in the first four sections will also be highly relevant when preparing for an internal influencing meeting.

3.10 CHAPTER 3 IN A NUTSHELL

To understand more about the other party during the negotiation:

- Ask open-ended questions
- Signal collaboration by starting to share information
- Explore options.

Here are five key indicators that can help you adapt your approach to negotiation in the most effective way:

- Your own negotiation style
- The negotiation style of the other party
- Cultural elements
- The balance of power in the negotiation
- The analysis of the Kraljič matrix.

A quick formula to evaluate the power balance in negotiations is to ask yourself:

- Which are the strengths of the two parties' BATNAs?
- Who has the most to lose, if you're not able to reach an agreement?

Once you have answered these, remember:

- To change the situation, or at least influence the other party's perception that you have less to lose and they have more to lose
- You have more power than you think.

Four key messages regarding emotions in a negotiation:

- Make sure you use both rational and emotional messages during the negotiation
- Show your emotions in a balanced way
- Learn to control your emotions
- Work on the 5 Core Concerns to build positive emotions.

To build a strong first impression, consider:

- Your written communication style
- Your nonverbal communication style
- Your tone of voice
- Your appearance
- Your ability to establish credibility while conveying genuine interest in the other party.

To build a rapport and create a basis for a better relationship with your stakeholders:

- Look for similarities
- Make effective compliments
- Use the technique of mirroring.

If you want to be perceived as more trustworthy by your counterpart, increase your Credibility, Reliability and Intimacy while decreasing your Self-Orientation (the four elements of the Trust Equation).

We also looked at a simple methodology to prepare for a negotiation, with an overview of some of the key questions to ask ourselves.

CHAPTER 4

CREATING VALUE IN NEGOTIATION

4.1 GATHERING INFORMATION DURING A NEGOTIATION

Should a good negotiator focus on delivering information or receiving information?

As you have probably guessed, a strong negotiator focuses more on receiving information than on delivering information. Information is power, and you want to get as much as possible of this information. Now, what can you do to encourage the other party to give you more information?

First, **create a climate of trust**. One of the things that you can do to create a climate of trust is share some information. It may even be something which is not related to the negotiation, such as 'I did not sleep much last night because my child was crying most of the night' or sharing some publicly available information. This type of action conveys to the other party that you trust them enough to share some information, even something personal.

Another key element of information exploration is **asking questions**. The challenge is that your counterpart may not want to answer them. It is important to ask these with a real sense of curiosity. When questions are asked in a genuine effort to understand the other party, then the reaction is different. Another way to increase your chances of a reply is to offer a convincing explanation before your question, such as: 'In order to better explain the situation to our planning team, can you please clarify your proposal regarding forecast exchanges?'. Another important skill when asking questions is not to limit ourselves to the initial question, but to ask follow-up questions that will increase the usefulness of the initial answer. Get used to asking in-depth follow-up questions, using a 'funnel approach' where each question becomes more specific.

A final source of information comes from **how the information is exchanged**. So, looking at the other person's tone of voice, body language, and level of resistance when you're discussing each topic provides you with valuable information about their interests and priorities.

4.2 EXPLOITING DIFFERENCES IN NEGOTIATION

As you approach a negotiation, do you tell yourself that common interests are an opportunity and differences are a source of conflict?

Well, I encourage you to reconsider your beliefs. In reality, the **differences between parties are often an opportunity to create a better outcome for both**. Let me give you two examples where the two parties' companies have different preferences and valuations, along with different preferred timing.

Preferences and valuations. In negotiations between buyers and sellers, I often see that the cost is a major driver for the buyer, while the seller may have other preferences, such as more volume or a longer-term contract. A simple way to create value would then be to agree a lower price for a bigger volume or a longer-term contract.

Time preferences. In one of my previous jobs, the company I worked for was trying to launch a new product. The biggest cost for this product was the active pharmaceutical ingredient (API). I asked the supplier to offer me a very competitive price in order to be able to successfully launch the product, but the supplier told me, 'I am sorry, but the price you ask is too low. There is no way that I can match your expectations.'

In the meantime, we worked on something else until November. This time, it was that same supplier that called me: 'I have a problem, because this year I will not reach my year-end bonus. I am short on volume, and I see that you have a big order for us in January. If you are able to move this order from January of next year to December of this year, then I will give you the price that you asked for the new API.' As you have probably understood, I had an interest in obtaining a long-term competitive price for the new product, while my supplier had an interest in increasing the short-term volume in order to reach his own targets. **Differences in time preferences can thus enable value creation**. You may also see that there is sometimes a conflict between personal and company interest in negotiation.

The key idea you should retain from these two examples is that differences are a great opportunity to create value in negotiation. **You should therefore be looking for elements of value that are important to one party and not the other, and vice versa**.

Another opportunity to create value is when people have different expectations about the future, something we will explore in the next paragraph.

4.3 CONTINGENCY AGREEMENTS

Were you ever confronted with a negotiation situation where the parties had different views about the future?

In my negotiation consulting activity, I often notice that the two negotiating parties have different views about the future. Usually, they try to argue and attempt to persuade the other party that they are right. A better way to resolve these kinds of differences is to establish a contingency agreement, which means that part of the compensation or any other negotiable item will be linked to something that is going to happen in the future. A bonus, a penalty, and a volume rebate are typical examples of a contingency agreement. If a customer buys 100 tonnes of product, they get a rebate; however, they will not get this rebate if they fail to buy the agreed volume. Let's see an example.

A large IT company was trying to acquire a small boutique IT company. When the parties had to agree on the amount of the acquisition, there was a problem. The owner of the small company believed that his company was going to grow by 20% every year, while the large IT company, although they appreciated the small company, believed that they were only going to grow by 5% each year. As a result, the two parties had very different expectations about the acquisition price. **When you have different views about the future, you can reach an agreement by making a contingency agreement**. In such an agreement, there will be a part of the deal that is linked to future results. For instance, the amount of money that goes to the small company will depend on the sales after a year and the profits after three years. In this way, both parties will be more inclined to close the deal.

A contingency agreement can also be used to spot a liar. When you believe that your counterpart is making a claim that does not reflect reality, request an element of variable compensation linked to this element. For instance, if a supplier claims to have 100% quality, ask them to accept penalties if there are quality issues and see their reaction.

When you have different views about the future with your negotiation counterpart or if you want to spot a liar, **make a contingency agreement where a part of the final outcome will be linked to something that is going to happen in the future**.

4.4 ENHANCING YOUR QUESTIONING ABILITY

When you want to influence someone, should you use questions or arguments?

When we use arguments, the acceptance rate of the counterpart is 24%, while when we use questions, the acceptance rate is 42%. This is something French philosopher Blaise Pascal already understood in the 17th century, when he said that '**People are usually more convinced by reasons they discovered themselves than by those found by others**.'

Now that we are clear on the power of questions to effectively negotiate and influence, let me share three techniques that can help you pose better questions.

1. **Prepare your questions in advance**: When you reflect and prepare your questions, they are likely to be better. Ask yourself: What is my objective with this question? Do I want to discover interests or maybe validate my hypothesis? This will help you consider how to properly phrase your question.

2. **Balance open and closed questions**: Most of the time you want to use open-ended questions, particularly 'How' and 'What' questions (see 4.1). Closed questions are used less frequently, usually making up 20–25% of the total. They also have an important role in the interaction, such as gaining confirmation, summarising a point and moving on to the next topic.

3. **Use probing questions**: A probing question goes deeper to get more details. Too often, I see negotiators moving from one open-ended question to another, while failing

to ask the follow-up question that would give them more details on an important matter. To be even more effective, make sure to combine your persistence with curiosity, i.e. with a sincere willingness to understand your counterpart.

Now we understand how critical it is to ask the right questions. To be fully effective, this has to be combined with strong listening skills.

4.5 HOW GOOD ARE YOUR LISTENING SKILLS?

Are you a good listener?

According to research from Accenture,[1] you are likely to reply to this question with a 'Yes!' Their survey found that 96% of people believe themselves to be good listeners, even if the majority (98 percent) spend part of their workday multi-tasking, including when in meetings. Too often people don't listen with focus and attention, which impacts respect shown and quality of information gained. Another study[2] interviewed over 8,000 people and asked them: 'In terms of listening skills, as compared with your colleagues, are you better, worse, or equal?'. And almost all of them responded that they were either just as good or better than their colleagues, which of course is unlikely.

In a survey I conducted with over 100 Procurement professionals with at least five years of experience, active listening was ranked second in terms of strength among 20 key behaviours of effective negotiators. On the other hand, when I run workshops for Salespeople, I consistently receive the feedback that Procurement people are bad listeners. There seems to be a mismatch between how good we think our listening skills are, and how good they *really* are.

The key message is that you may want to start working on your active listening skills. Four techniques to get you started:

---

1   Accenture Research, #ListenLearnLead (2015).
2   D. P. Nolan and E. T. Anderson, *Applied Operational Excellence for the Oil, Gas, and Process Industries* (Gulf Professional Publishing, 2015).

- **Refrain from thinking about your own response**. Rather than starting to prepare your response while the other person is talking, listen with curiosity and just focus on what they are saying.
- **Pause before replying**. Instead of aiming to reply as quickly as possible, make it a habit to wait a couple of seconds before replying. In such a way, you will show respect to your counterpart and have a couple of extra seconds to reflect and understand the other, to gain clarification if needed, and only then move forward. Resist the tendency to start your reply with a counterargument.
- **Repeat the last 1–3 words** (or last critical words), ideally with a question mark. The key ability is to choose what is significant or what you want to know more about.
- **Use paraphrasing**. This is about expressing the meaning of what you have heard with different words in a shorter way. More insights into paraphrasing will be covered in our next paragraph.

4.6 ACTIVE LISTENING – PARAPHRASING

Active listening is a core competency for a negotiator. You have probably already heard a number of times that listening is important. In fact, a common saying is that we have two ears and one mouth, and we want to use them accordingly. Therefore, in an effective negotiation, plan to spend twice as much time listening than talking.

Let's focus on one skill that can help you to be more effective in negotiation as well as improve your listening skills. We want to **learn how to paraphrase well**. Paraphrasing is about saying what you have heard in a shorter way, with a different choice of words, while reflecting the same meaning. This is particularly important when you are dealing with people from different cultures, or maybe people with a basic level of English, to ensure that you understood the message that they wanted to convey.

Let's use an example to understand this better. Imagine how you would paraphrase the following sentence:

'Well, last week I was at the Nestlé Global Headquarters to run two workshops on gender differences in negotiation on the occasion of International Women's Day. I had very nice participants and two very interactive sessions. I very much enjoyed the event.'

Now, let's start by looking at ineffective paraphrasing. An excessively long example may go: 'Oh, so you were at Nestlé to talk about gender differences in negotiation on International Women's Day and you had two good sessions.' Here, we are pretty much repeating what we heard almost word for word, which is too much. On the other hand, a too-short response may be something like, 'Oh, you were teaching last week.'

So, a better way to paraphrase can be, 'Okay, so, you were running workshops at Nestlé last week for International Women's Day.' That's the kind of effective paraphrasing you want to achieve, since it is concise and captures the key elements of the message you received.

Also watch out for some of the typical mistakes we make when paraphrasing: adding our own interpretations, bringing in our own autobiography, making it too long, judging, giving advice, providing solutions.

Make sure to practice this powerful technique in your professional and private life, as you will see an immediate impact on your listening skills.

4.7 APPLYING EMPATHIC LISTENING

Were you ever confronted with strong emotions during a negotiation?

As a Procurement executive, I have often seen such emotions, particularly managing conflicts or when negotiating with business owners. When emotions run high, whether in business or in private life, a powerful tool is to **use empathic listening**. The core idea is to try capturing the emotion that the other person is feeling.

Now, to effectively use empathic listening, **having the right attitude** is essential. This involves being fully available, listening with a willingness to understand, suspending your own thoughts and judgements and accepting the other person's feelings, even if they are different from yours.

Once you have the right attitude, then **the skills required will be to identify and label the emotion or feeling that the other person is experiencing at that moment**. You also start the sentence with a few words indicating that you are not sure if you got it right. So your message will go like this: 'It seems to me that you are frustrated by this situation.' Or you may say, 'It looks like you are disappointed by the behaviour of your colleagues.' By naming their feelings, you move the conversation to the emotional level. And even if you get the feeling wrong, you are likely to be corrected by the other person, who is going to mention the real emotion that they are feeling.

4.8 CHAPTER 4 IN A NUTSHELL

To gather information during a negotiation:

- Create a climate of trust
- Ask questions with a real sense of curiosity
- Pay attention to how information is being exchanged.

Look for differences between both sides, then you will be able to create value for both parties. Differences may include access to resources, different capabilities, different taxation regimes, future expectations, different interests and priorities, time preferences, and different attitudes towards risk.

To improve your ability to ask questions:

- Prepare your questions in advance
- Balance open and closed questions
- Use probing questions.

To become a better listener:

- Refrain from thinking about your own responses
- Pause before replying
- Repeat the last 1–3 words
- Use paraphrasing.

To effectively use empathic listening:

- Have a non-judgemental and open attitude
- Try to identify the feeling that the other person is experiencing and convey it to them.

CHAPTER 5

CLAIMING VALUE IN NEGOTIATION

5.1 MAKING THE FIRST OFFER IN A NEGOTIATION

Who do you think should make the first offer in a negotiation?

I was in the Middle East teaching at the London Business School when working on this section. When you enter a market to buy (for example) a carpet, the general rule is to let the other party come up with a price first. If you make the first offer without understanding the local market, you may end up offering too much and getting an overpriced carpet. This is important to remember, especially when you are going to a place where you are unfamiliar with the local conditions and do not know the market.

Here is a different perspective: **It may be better for you if you share the first number in a negotiation, provided that you know the market.**

To explain this idea, I want to introduce you to the concept of anchoring. Much of the initial research on anchoring comes from Daniel Kahneman and Amos Tversky. It is one of the theories that contributed to Daniel Kahneman winning the Nobel Prize in Economics in 2002. The core idea of the application of anchoring to negotiation is that the first number used in a negotiation sets the reference (an anchor) for the discussion and shapes the behaviour of the counterpart.

A classic example was run by Kahneman and Tversky.[1] They had a wheel of fortune in a conference room with numbers between zero and 100, while the wheel was rigged to land only on numbers 10 and 65. As the wheel was turned, they asked participants to guess the percentage of African countries that are part of the United Nations (UN). When the number on the wheel of fortune was 65, the respondents estimated a high percentage of African countries in the UN, with an average of 45%. When the number was 10, participants estimated a low percentage of African countries in the UN, with an average of 25%. A random number in the wheel of fortune was leading people to make different assumptions. As you can imagine, the anchoring effect is stronger when people are not well prepared. (By the way, at the time of the study, the percentage of African countries in the UN was 42%.)

If we translate this study into the field of negotiation, we can gain an advantage by being the one that suggests the first number during the negotiation process. Our initial offer becomes a reference or an 'anchor' for the negotiation, which will influence the reply of your counterpart and have an impact on the overall result.

Now you may ask yourself, should I always be the one making the first offer?

---

1   D. Kahneman, *Thinking, Fast and Slow* (Farrar, Straus and Giroux, 2011).

Not always. Only if you are well prepared and know the market well. If you do not know the market and make the first offer, you may cnd up giving a numbcr that is too high or too low and which could result in either a bad deal or a loss of credibility with an offer that is too extreme.

My advice is **to be well prepared and research the market**, so that you can make the first offer and take advantage of the powerful anchoring principle. This will enable you to influence the negotiating range in your favour and therefore the outcome of your negotiations. When you do not have sufficient information, it does not mean that you want them to anchor. If they are competent, they will then set the amount in their favour. Your job instead is to find ways to gather relevant information, either before or during the negotiation, so that you have enough information to make the first offer.

To conclude, let me give you five pieces of advice to leverage the power of anchoring effectively:

1. **Be well prepared**. When you are well prepared, you can make an effective anchor, without giving a number which is too high or too low. This will also help you to be less influenced if the other party is making the first offer.
2. **Support your anchor with an explanation**. The more you are able to come up with a rational and lengthy explanation on how you come up with that number, the more your anchor will appear credible. In addition, make sure not only to give a number but also to define the issues that are being discussed. An effective salesperson will take the opportunity to make the first offer, which could include

an expanded scope of services, geographical expansions and other growth opportunities.

3. **Your anchor should be a bit more aggressive than the limit of the other party**. If you are buying a house and you believe that the seller will not sell the house below 500,000 EUR, you should probably offer 430,000 EUR or 455,000 EUR so that you can push the other party to their limits without appearing unreasonable.

4. **Use unrounded numbers**. Selling your motorbike at 11,650 EUR will make the number seem much more professional and firmer.

5. **Continue the micro-anchoring during the negotiation process**. This involves continuing to repeat your number rather than the counterpart's own number during the negotiation process, so that your number becomes the reference.

5.2 EFFECTIVE TECHNIQUES
IN CONCESSION-MAKING

An important component in reaching an agreement in negotiation is making concessions. What are the most effective concession-making techniques?

Let me share my four favourites with you.

The first one is to **make the other party work for everything they get**. One of the problems that I often see in my consulting or training activity is that my clients make concessions too quickly. 'Is it possible to be paid in cash?' 'Well, yeah, that is no problem. That is something that we can do. I will find a solution for you.' Now, once you make the concession so easily, then the other person is not going to value the concession. So ensure that you make them work before giving the concession, and explain that you are really making an effort in order to offer it.

The second one is to **make smaller concessions over time**. Compare these two concessions patterns (i.e. the different prices that you would offer during a negotiation):

Pattern 1: 40 – 50 – 60 – 70 – 80 …
Pattern 2: 40 – 45 – 47 – 47.5 – 47.7 – 47.9 …

As you can see, pattern 2 is much more effective as you are showing that you are getting closer and closer to your limits.

The third is to **prepare a list of giveaways**. You should bring to the negotiation table not only the topics that you want to win, but also other topics that are not important to you and that you are prepared to give away. Let's imagine that you want to win four different topics in a negotiation. If you want to discuss only these four topics, you are unlikely to win them all. A more effective way is to bring eight topics to the negotiation table and let the other party win at some of these, while you win the four that you really care about. The giveaways will then enable you to trade concessions. You can then get what you want while having a more satisfied counterpart and a better negotiation climate.

The fourth way is to **make trades**. It starts with an understanding of the value that the parties associate with the different negotiable items and the identification of the topics that have high value for one of the parties and low value for another. You can then ask for something of high value to you while giving something of lower value to you in return, by using the famous sentence: '**If you..., then we...**'. When making trades, it is important to keep the right order. First talk about what you expect from them, then indicate what you are prepared to give back. Otherwise, they may take the first part without giving you the second. A final tip about making trades: Do not overuse them. Sometimes you need to make concessions, other times you make trades. If you *always* make trades, if everything you do is conditional, then it's difficult to build trust and to strengthen the relationship with the counterpart.

5.3 STRENGTHENING OUR POWER IN NEGOTIATION

Who has more power in negotiations, the buyer or the seller?

When Tesco, Carrefour, or other large retailers meet with their smaller suppliers, they tend to be quite harsh. They make a lot of demands; they give little time for the meetings, and they are quite firm in their requests because they have the power. In those situations, the buyer has the power. On the other hand, when there are shortages of raw materials, clearly the seller has the power.

In general, there is no fixed rule. **The buyer or the seller may have more power, depending on the context, the situation, and the market**. The relationship between a buyer and a seller is somewhere between a continuum where on one side, there is a monopoly, and on the other side, there is a commodity. So, the job of a seller is to be perceived by the buyer as a monopoly. And the job of the buyer is to be able to treat every seller as a commodity supplier.

Now, if you are a seller, what can you do to strengthen your power? You may want to work on your **differentiation strategy** and identify something which makes you unique. This may be **technology, branding, or a unique business model**. For instance, if you look at the large fast-moving consumer goods companies, like Procter & Gamble or Nestlé, they invest a substantial amount of money in marketing, so that they build a relationship with the consumers. And this gives them more power when they negotiate with the retailers.

If you are a buyer, the most typical strategy to increase your power is to build a number of alternatives. A way to make it easy to build alternatives is to **reduce the barrier**

to qualify new suppliers. This may be, for instance, using performance specifications rather than detailed specifications. You may also want to have some sort of **benchmark** to build a good understanding of the market. **Knowledge is also a source of power**, and if you do not have the knowledge, you can get it from somewhere else. For instance, if you are negotiating with Microsoft every three years, it may be more effective to hire an external consultant that will guide you to negotiate rather than trying to build all the knowledge yourself.

In more general terms, your biggest source of power will be your ability to add value to your counterpart!

5.4 NEGOTIATING STYLES AND CONFLICT MANAGEMENT

The way we are going to approach conflicts will depend on how much focus we have on two key dimensions: the importance of the relationship with our counterpart and our own agenda/goals/expectations. Then depending on how we balance those two elements, we will have five different styles of dealing with conflict.

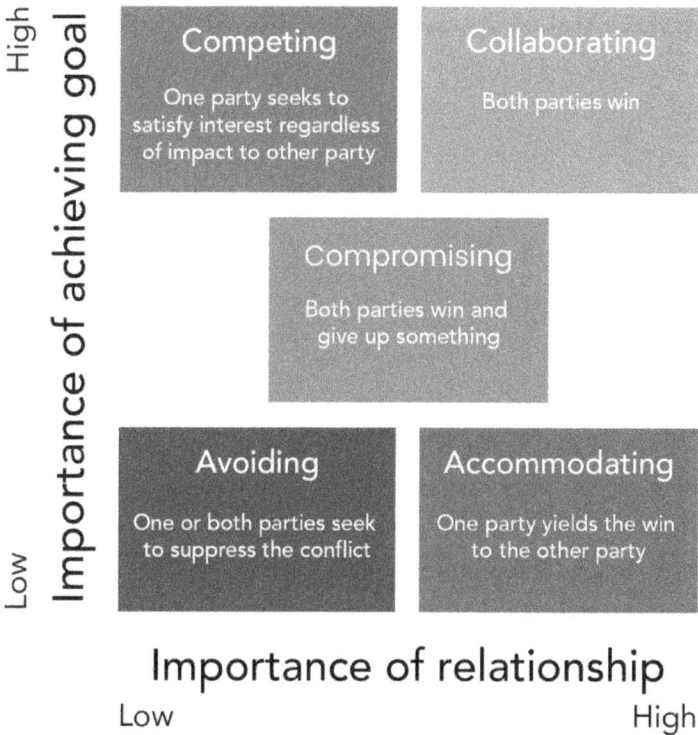

Competing
One party seeks to satisfy interest regardless of impact to other party

Collaborating
Both parties win

Compromising
Both parties win and give up something

Avoiding
One or both parties seek to suppress the conflict

Accommodating
One party yields the win to the other party

High — Importance of achieving goal — **Low**

Importance of relationship
Low   High

To understand those five styles, consider a pragmatic example. Let's say that it is Saturday night. You are going to have a discussion with your partner about what to do tonight, and you are very keen to watch a new movie. Let's now apply the five different styles to this situation.

If you are using a **competing style**, then you are likely to say, 'Tonight, I would really like to go and watch this new movie.' On the other hand, if you are using **an accommodating style**, then you are likely to say, 'Well, let's do whatever you want.' If you use an **avoidant style**, you are not even going to talk about the facts of going out. In a **collaborating style**, you will first say, 'Well, I would very much like to go and watch this new movie tonight. On the other hand, I want to make sure that we also do something that you like. What are you keen to do?'. To conclude, when using the **compromising style**, the exchange may go: 'Well, I would like to go to the cinema and watch this new movie, but you would prefer to stay home. Okay, let's watch a movie on Netflix together.'

Now that we understand those five styles, here are three key messages that can help you put the concepts together.

First, **there is no right or wrong style**, as the right style will depend on the situation. The way you manage a conflict in a one-off negotiation may be different from the way you manage it in an ongoing business relationship. You should choose your style to strategically fit the situation.

Second, you **want to build flexibility** in how you manage conflicts. You may want to be able to use different styles for different types of situations. To learn a bit more about your own style, you may even want to take a conflict management test. (There are a number of these online, with the most popular being the Thomas-Kilmann test and the Kraybill test.) For a comprehensive comparison of assessment tools, you may want to check out this article.[2] By doing a test, you will gain a better understanding about your natural way to deal with conflict, along with the styles you should develop to build flexibility.

The third way is to **be careful with the style that you naturally tend to use when your emotions get out of hand**, because it is in those types of situations we tend to do or say things we later regret.

2   R. A. Friedman et al., "What Goes Around Comes Around: The Impact of Personal Conflict Style on Work Conflict and Stress," *The International Journal of Conflict Management* 11, no.1 (2000): 32–55.

5.5 DEALING WITH DEADLOCKS IN BUSINESS NEGOTIATIONS

Have you ever been in a situation where you were negotiating with another party and the deal was just not moving forward?

This is an example of a deadlock, where it seems that you are not going to be able to reach an agreement.

For example, consider this situation from the very beginning of my career. I was trying to establish a long-term agreement with a chemical supplier, which was in discord with the market practices. The market was operating with monthly price negotiations, and we wanted to engage in a long-term agreement. The salesperson and I had been negotiating for seven months trying to reach an agreement. We were not really moving forward. So in that type of situation, what can one do to prevent getting stuck?

First, **add new elements**. What could you bring into the agreement that will enable you to open new avenues and therefore get out of the deadlock? In this specific case, we introduced some risk management mechanisms so that whenever the market fluctuated too much, the negotiating parties would mitigate their losses.

The second way is to **prepare their victory speech**. As you look for solutions to move out of the deadlock, try to think, 'What could I propose that will make the deal look like a victory for them?'. How could we shape the proposal so that they would go to their stakeholders and say, 'Yes, we had a successful outcome. It was a big achievement for us.'? In this specific case, for instance, we agreed that they could use our brand name in their internal communications and have an article in their internal magazine, so that they could claim that they had established a global agreement with a prestigious customer.

The third way is to **change the players**. Often you are in a deadlock because your relationship with the person you are negotiating with is confrontational. In my specific example, the relationship with the salesperson was very good. The problem was the level of seniority, which was inadequate to sign such a big agreement. The way to change the negotiation dynamics was to bring seniority into the negotiating team so that both sides of the management would be part of the negotiation, and they could agree to these substantial changes.

5.6 NEGOTIATION TACTICS WITH NO NEGATIVE IMPACT ON RELATIONSHIP

A number of negotiation tactics (power tactics, time tactics…) are not likely to be appreciated by the other party. I want to take you through three tactics that you can use that will not impact the relationship with your negotiation counterpart.

One of my favourites is the **hot air balloon**. The idea of the hot air balloon is to use a hypothetical question to explore ideas without making a firm commitment. The typical structure of this tactic is the use of 'what if'. What if we explored using a different product? What if we changed our agreement regarding intellectual property? The benefit of this tactic is that you get an idea about what is important for the other party without making a firm commitment to go ahead on a specific topic.

A second simple tactic that you can use is the **time out**. Pausing the negotiation can be a way to ensure the relationship isn't impacted. For instance, if emotions are rising, and you want to avoid the possibility that the negotiation derails, it is best to take some time out. This can be a powerful tool to realign with your team in case there are new elements that have shown up in the negotiations, and as a team, you want to decide the appropriate next steps.

The third tactic is the **salami tactic**. The idea is that you do not give away something in one shot, but piece by piece instead. And every time you make a concession, you get something in return. For instance, let us assume that you are prepared to make a three-year contract that is highly valuable for the other party. Rather than giving it away immediately, what you do is start with a one-year contract, which you negotiate hard for. Then you ask, 'What are you prepared to offer to me if I give you a two-year contract?'. Once you receive something in return, you may say: 'It looks like you value a longer-term relationship. If we could go for a three-year contract, what would you be able to offer me?'.

5.7 USING THE LIMITED AUTHORITY TACTIC

During a negotiation, have you ever experienced when your counterpart tells you, 'Well, let me review your proposal with my boss.'

It is a typical example of 'the limited authority' tactic, because it gives the individual more time to review your proposal and then come back to you asking for additional concessions. When somebody uses this tactic, the most effective reply is to tell them, 'Listen, I want to negotiate with the decision-maker. If you are the decision-maker, fine. If you are not, next time I will negotiate directly with your boss.' That is a good way to ensure the other person is not going to keep using this tactic again.

An even better approach is to clarify the level of authority of your counterpart even before the negotiation starts. As part of the clarification of the process (agenda, timing, participants…), you want to ensure that you involve the right people at the negotiation table. If it is not possible to bring the decision-maker to the negotiation table, then proceed with the awareness that the person you are negotiating with does not have, or claims not to have, the final authority.

Should you use the limited authority tactic? There are certainly advantages in going into a negotiation without the full authority (even if you are the CEO!). For instance, it may give you more time to align with the rest of the organisation and evaluate the proposed agreement. Just be careful about the impact that the use of such a tactic would have on the relationship. If you choose to use it, make sure your stakeholders are aware and prepared with the necessary background in case they receive a call on the case being negotiated asking for their decision.

5.8 CHAPTER 5 IN A NUTSHELL

To leverage the power of anchoring effectively:

- Be well prepared
- Support your anchor with an explanation
- Ensure your anchor is a bit more aggressive than the limit of the other party
- Use unrounded numbers
- Continue repeating your number during the negotiation, rather than the counterpart number.

Four ideas that can help you in concession-making:

- Make the other party work for everything they get
- Make smaller concessions over time
- Prepare a list of giveaways
- Make trades.

If you are a seller, your aim is to become a monopoly in the eyes of the buyer. If you are a buyer, your aim is to be able to treat every seller as a commodity supplier.

We have seen five ways to deal with conflict along with three key messages:

- There is no right or wrong style
- We want to build flexibility so that we can use the right style for the right situation
- We want to be careful with the style that we tend to use when our emotions get out of hand.

To get out of the deadlock, there are three ideas you can apply:

- Add new elements
- Prepare their victory speech
- Change the players.

Three tactics that do not have a negative impact on the relationship are:

- Hot air balloon
- Time out
- Salami tactic.

Going into a negotiation without full authority may give you more time to align with the rest of the organisation and evaluate the proposed agreement.

CHAPTER 6

VIRTUAL NEGOTIATIONS

6.1 NEGOTIATING OVER EMAIL

Think about it: In the past three months, how often have you negotiated via email?

The number of email negotiations have certainly increased in the last few years and it is important to master this skill.

You are probably already familiar with some of the advantages and disadvantages of email negotiations. For instance, some of the advantages include that it is **less stressful, you can hide your emotions, you have more time to think**. On the other hand, there are some disadvantages. For instance, **it takes more time to reach an agreement, there is a higher risk of misunderstanding and there is also a tendency to be more competitive**. In fact, based on a study from Leigh Thompson, a professor at Kellogg's, the tendency to be more competitive is up to eight times higher in email negotiation compared to face-to-face negotiation.[1]

Recognising those advantages and disadvantages, let me share with you three points that can help you to become more effective.

---

1   L. Thompson, *The Truth About Negotiations* (Pearson Prentice Hall Business, 2008).

1. **Summarise key topics and next steps**. There's a higher risk of misunderstanding; therefore, on a regular basis, it is important to summarise what has been discussed and what has been agreed. Writing this summary is also an opportunity to frame the information in the ways that are more beneficial to you. You may want to indicate the direction of future discussions or ask some questions that you forgot to ask in the previous exchange.

2. **Do not make assumptions; ask questions**. During email exchanges, the information may not be fully clear. The evidence is that there is a much greater chance of being misunderstood even when you think what you have said is clear (and vice versa). Rather than making assumptions about the other party's intention and pretending that you have understood the ambiguous message, it is better to be straightforward and ask for clarifications. This avoids a possibility of the negotiations going in the wrong direction during the email exchange.

3. **When receiving an email, do not reply immediately**. One of the benefits of email negotiation is that it gives you time to think, so you should therefore take this opportunity to reflect on the message. In particular if the email that you receive is upsetting you, resist the tendency to reply immediately, as this could result in derailing the negotiation and ending up on a difficult path. The speed at which you reply to an email gives a signal to the other party. If you reply too quickly, you probably sound too eager; however, if you reply too slowly, this is going to affect the trust that the other person may have in you.

6.2 TELEPHONE NEGOTIATIONS

Is there any difference between face-to-face negotiations and telephone negotiations? As you probably correctly guessed, yes, there are a few differences.

Here are five tips that can help you to be more effective in telephone negotiations.

1. **Take some time to prepare**. Somehow, we consider the face-to-face negotiation as real, while the ones by telephone are considered less important. As a result, we often forget to prepare.
2. **Initiate the call**. Do not get trapped into receiving a call from a customer or a supplier, then immediately start to negotiate. Instead, tell them that you are going to call them back. Then you have the time to prepare and have all your facts and figures close to you.
3. **Do not check your emails**. We all have the temptation to multitask. As we are negotiating on the phone, if we notice an email from our boss, then we may end up reading the message. This is very common, and also very dangerous. We know that listening is a core competency for negotiators, so keep distractions away and be focused on the call.
4. **Take more notes**. Since you cannot count on your visual memory to recall the conversation, make sure that you take extensive notes so that you can better remember what was discussed on the call. If their message is not clear, make sure to follow up with questions to clarify and confirm understanding.

5. **Pay attention to your voice**. There is a direct correlation between the way you speak and the credibility of your message. Some of the most important tips include speaking with a lower pitch (deeper voice), using a falling intonation (making sure that the intonation of your voice drops at the end of the sentence) and avoiding hesitations and filler words. See paragraph 12.7 for more details.

6.3 DEALING WITH VIRTUAL NEGOTIATION CHALLENGES

Following the COVID-19 crisis, the number of virtual negotiations has sharply increased. Are you getting the most from those virtual negotiations? I want to address three typical challenges that we have during virtual negotiations and what you can do to deal with them.

1. **It is easy to get distracted**. To deal with it, switch off email notifications and mute or keep your phone away. Also, focus on taking more notes. This enables you to concentrate on what is being discussed, and you will also be able to recall the points later. To reduce the risk of distraction, make sure to schedule shorter and more frequent meetings so that it is easier to stay focused.

2. **Lack of colocation with your team members during the preparation phase and during the negotiation**. To deal with this, you may want to start the preparation process at an earlier stage, because it is going to take longer to align. You cannot count on meeting your colleagues at the coffee machine or at the cafeteria, or casually discussing the issues at their office. As you align, also assign specific roles to each negotiation participant so that it is clear what each person is going to do during the negotiation. Make sure you also agree on a simple way to continue to exchange offline (e.g. via a direct messaging platform) so that you can check how the other people feel about the current negotiation. Another piece of advice is to schedule regular breaks during your meetings, so that

you can discuss with your team members and understand if you are all still on the same page.

3. **It is more difficult to build trust and rapport.** To deal with this challenge, make sure that you make a deliberate effort to invest in the relationship. At the beginning of the meeting, take some time to connect, maybe share some positive emotion and personal stories, and use plural pronouns like we/us/ours rather than you and I. This helps to create a better rapport. Regarding trust-building, we should recognise an important difference: In face-to-face negotiations, trust-building is emotional, while in virtual negotiations, trust-building is cognitive. As a result, you will build trust through your behaviour during the negotiation.

6.4 CHOOSING THE RIGHT COMMUNICATION TOOLS FOR VIRTUAL NEGOTIATIONS

How do you reliably choose the right communication tool for virtual negotiations?

For a few years, videoconferencing has become the standard tool for virtual negotiation. But is it always the right tool? It's true that the richer the communication medium, the easier it is to exchange information and build trust. But let me give you three perspectives regarding the right choice of virtual communication tool.

1. **What is the purpose that you want to achieve?** For instance, a video conference is best if you want to build rapport with the other person. A phone call is appropriate for a quick clarification. An email is probably right for a detailed proposal. A text message is perhaps a way to move forward quicker, while still communicating in writing.
2. **What is the context of the negotiation?** You may want to choose a richer information tool, such as video conferencing, if you are dealing with an important negotiation or a complex multi-party negotiation. When you have a power or information disadvantage, or even if you are in a competitive type of negotiation, choose a simple information tool like email.
3. **What kind of tools are effective?** A message I want you to keep in mind is that there are a number of virtual communication tools and, most of the time, you want to choose a combination. For instance, if you are in a difficult negotiation, maybe you want to start with a video

conference to set the scene, then send a detailed proposal via email, then give the other party some time to think, and then set up another video conference to discuss your proposal. Even during the video conference negotiation, you may want to continue to use other tools, such as exchanging text messages with your team members or with the counterpart's key contact person.

6.5 CHAPTER 6 IN A NUTSHELL

Three key ideas that can help you to be more effective in email negotiation:

- Summarise key topics and next steps on a regular basis
- Do not make assumptions; instead, clarify any ambiguous information
- Do not reply immediately to emails, but take the time to think it over.

There are five key elements that you want to keep in mind in telephone negotiations:

- Take time to prepare like for a face-to-face negotiation
- Initiate the call—do not be caught unprepared
- Do not look at your emails–focus on the call
- Take more notes to better remember what is being said
- Pay attention to your voice.

Three typical challenges that we have during virtual negotiations and what we can do to deal with them are:

- To avoid distractions, make sure your email and phone alerts are on mute and schedule shorter meetings
- To deal with lack of colocation with your team members, start the preparation phase earlier and establish the right internal communication tools to continue to be aligned
- To build trust and rapport, make a deliberate effort to invest time in the relationship and behave in a way that conveys trust.

Be clear on the objective that you want to achieve and the context of the negotiation, then choose the right combination of virtual communication tools to achieve your goals.

CHAPTER 7

PROCUREMENT AND SALES NEGOTIATIONS

7.1 FIGHTING A PRICE INCREASE

Imagine you are a buyer and a supplier asks you for a price increase. You might be tempted to ask: 'How can you justify the higher price?'. Even though this sounds like a good idea, it is not the best reply. As soon as you ask the supplier for a justification, you are already opening the door for a price rise and weakening your negotiation position.

Let me give you two more effective first responses to deal with such a request. If you want to use a more collaborative tone it can be something like, 'How can we work together to make sure that we are not going to have any price increase?'. If you want to set a more competitive tone, then insist: 'We are not going to accept any price increase!'.

If we go back to the anchoring theory that we have studied previously (see 5.1), there is an important difference between these possible replies. If you ask them to justify their price increase, you are reinforcing their anchor. If you ask for no increase, you are setting your own anchor at zero increase!

Assuming the supplier does not accept your proposal and keeps pushing for a price increase, here are five strategies that you can use to deal with their request:

1. **Look at the supplier's past behaviour.** For instance, when the raw material prices went down, did they actually offer you a price decrease or did the prices remain stable?

2. **Consider offering something in return for price stability.** For instance, we could offer a longer-term contract or additional business opportunities.

3. **Delay the increase.** If you are not able to block the request for a price increase you can try to implement it as late as possible. You may say something like, 'The final prices to our customer are fixed for this fiscal year. I am not in the position to authorise a price increase for this fiscal year.'

4. **Explore the option of giving a part of the business to another supplier.** If you believe that the price increase request is not justified and does not represent a market trend, you may want to shift part of the business to someone else. Remember that we educate our suppliers to behave in a certain way with us. If you never make bold moves, the supplier will feel comfortable continually asking for increases.

5. **Keep suppliers accountable to keep costs down.** Even if the markets are increasing, suppliers should be doing their part to keep costs down. Did they put some hedging in place? What is their sourcing strategy?

7.2 HOW TO 'CONDITION' A SUPPLIER

How do you 'condition' suppliers? What can you do to make sure that the supplier will give you the very best terms?

First, let me clarify what we mean by conditioning a supplier. It is about persuading your suppliers that you have certain expectations of them and that you need them to respond to you in a particular way. Here are three tips that will help you to condition the suppliers effectively:

1. **Highlight the opportunity**. If you choose to use 'positive conditioning', you can get suppliers motivated by talking about the fact that there are new markets, that there is growth potential, that you are open to change, and that you're working across business units with an increased scope.

2. **Highlight the challenge**. In this case, you use 'negative conditioning'. You would now focus on the fact that there is increased competition, that the competition includes low-cost suppliers coming from other markets, that your company is under financial pressure and you need the very best terms.

3. **Provide a strong and professional general impression**. Some of the factors that allow you to make a strong impression include your appearance, how you dress, your behaviour during calls or meetings, your attention to detail, the quality of the documents that you have, whether your company has a professional website, whether you track the data so that you have updated KPIs. This third element—your behaviour—is relevant with both positive and negative conditioning.

7.3 NEGOTIATING WITH PROCUREMENT

Across many industries, a number of negotiations that used to be led directly by the business are now managed by Procurement. When I run workshops for sales teams, participants regularly talk about the good times when the negotiations were taking place with the end user and how difficult it is now to negotiate with Procurement. If you often struggle to negotiate with Procurement, this paragraph is for you. To negotiate more effectively in this area, I have three strategies that can help you:

1. **The better the sales job, the easier the negotiation**. If you, as the salesperson, were able to convince your potential customer that you have the best solution—or even better, the *only* solution—then your negotiation with Procurement is going to be much easier.
2. **Bypass Procurement**. Go directly to the business, close the deal with them, and then confront Procurement with the 'fait accompli' (i.e. something that has already been decided before those affected hear about it). Of course, this is a competitive type of tactic that has an impact on the relationship. You therefore have to evaluate its application carefully, especially if you care about a good relationship with Procurement in the future.
3. **Remember that Procurement often has a focus on cost-saving**. You can use this information in two ways. Firstly, give yourself room for negotiation by asking for more than you are really expecting to obtain. In such a way, Procurement can claim some cost savings and you can still have a good deal. A second idea is to leverage

Procurement's focus on price to get something else that is even more valuable to you. For instance, you may trade any price concession to get a longer-term contract.

7.4 TYPICAL NEGOTIATION MISTAKES IN PROCUREMENT

Before becoming a Negotiation and Influencing Professor, I learnt these skills by working in Procurement for over 20 years with four leading multinationals. Let me share with you three typical mistakes that, in my experience, Procurement people often make:

1. **Over-focus on price compared to other interests in a negotiation**. This price focus comes from the way Procurement organisations have been measured for over 30 years. When the key performance indicator is cost saving, there is too much emphasis on price and other opportunities for value creation are lost.

2. **Fail to ask enough questions**. In a typical interaction between a seller and a buyer, the seller is the one who asks most of the questions whereas the buyer tends to make statements or arguments. Many Procurement managers think that this is the most effective way to win a negotiation. For a different perspective, imagine a job interview. You will notice that the person who asks the question is the one who leads the discussion.

3. **Emphasis on price, rather than volume and specifications as other ways to reduce cost**. A study from the consulting firm McKinsey actually indicates that 80% of the cost reduction opportunities come from volume and specifications, and only 20% from price.

Here are a couple of examples from my own experience, on **how to reduce cost based on specifications and volume**.

These examples assume that you are well-integrated with your business, are involved upfront, and have an in-depth knowledge of the kind of products that you are buying.

When working in the pharmaceutical industry, one of our key products had many different formulations across the world (for historical reasons). Rather than trying to buy the raw materials at a lower price, we chose to standardise the specification for this product, choosing the formulation that was effective for the patient, acceptable by regulators, and the lowest in cost. We ended up achieving a 50% lower cost for this product than the ones that we had in the past.

Another example is based on using volumes as a way to reduce cost (a technique often referred to in Procurement as 'demand management'). In one of my previous Procurement experiences, we spent large sums on consulting services. We could have tried to negotiate more with the consulting firms and get lower daily rates for the consulting services, although there is a limit on how much you can reduce those rates. A more effective approach was to work on the volume, i.e. on the amount of consulting services that we would purchase. We introduced a zero-budgeting approach, which means that each of the executives did not automatically have the same consulting budget as the previous year. Each consulting mandate had to be justified and approved by top management, based on specific business needs for that year. This approach drastically reduced the spend on consulting services.

7.5 CHAPTER 7 IN A NUTSHELL

If you want to fight a price increase:

- Start by firmly stating that you will not accept the increase
- Look at the supplier's past behaviour to see if an increase is justified
- Consider offering something in return for price stability
- Delay the price increase
- Explore the option of giving a part of the business to another supplier
- Keep the supplier accountable to keep costs down.

These are the three points to condition your suppliers:

- Highlight the opportunity for additional business
- Highlighting the challenge of risking the loss of business
- Provide a strong and professional general impression.

These are the key points to negotiate with Procurement:

- Do a better sales job. Once the company really wants you, the negotiation will be easier.
- Bypass Procurement and go directly to the business, while considering the impact on the relationship with your Procurement counterpart.
- Use Procurement's strong interest in cost savings to get what you want, while ensuring that they are satisfied.

If you are on the Sales side, remember the three typical mistakes by Procurement people (over-focus on price compared to other interests in a negotiation, failing to ask enough questions, and an emphasis on price, compared to volume and specifications as other ways to reduce cost). Then, take corrective actions based on this information. If you are on the Procurement side, then you can be more effective by:

- Looking at all the interests in a negotiation (not only price)
- Asking more questions rather than just making statements
- Exploring opportunities to reduce cost via volume and specifications (not only price).

CHAPTER 8

BROADENING YOUR NEGOTIATION SKILLS

8.1 DEFINING THE NEGOTIATION PROCESS

Let me share some inspiration from Harvard Professor Deepak Malhotra.[1] Imagine a situation: You are a salesperson, and you have been negotiating with someone for a few months. You still have a few concessions that you can make. They are painful, but you are prepared to make them if this is going to enable you to close the deal. You therefore decide to make these concessions and put forward your best proposal. And the person on the other side tells you, 'Well, thank you very much for making this offer. Let me review it with my boss.'

Guess what? The negotiation is probably not over. They are going to come back with additional requests and you will have nothing else to give. This is a typical example of the problems we may experience when not defining the negotiation process.

---

1   "Process Before Substance", video by D. Malhotra, posted March 8, 2020, by Deepak Malhotra. YouTube, 3 minutes, https://www.youtube.com/watch?v=f1ORmtdpJpk

My key advice is to **negotiate the process before you negotiate the substance.**

Here are some examples of the type of questions that you can use to negotiate the process: If we want to make a decision by this date, how many meetings are we going to have? Will they be physical or virtual? Who will be participating in these meetings? Will the persons attending the meeting have authority to make a deal or will they have to defer to somebody else? What are some of the factors that may slow things down? Speed them up? What is the objective and agenda of the next meeting? Where will it take place?

When you think about defining the process, also keep in mind a couple of other points. If you want to claim value, i.e. if you want to get the best for yourself, then **you can shape the process to your advantage**, e.g. organise the meeting agenda to better meet your needs. If instead you want to create value and build a better long-term relationship, then go for a joint definition of the agenda, including transparency and clearer ground rules. Research[2] indicates that negotiators are more satisfied with the outcome of a negotiation if this outcome has been reached through a fair process.

---

2   J.R. Curhan, H.A. Elfenbein and H. Xu, "What Do People Value When They Negotiate? Mapping the Domain of Subjective Value in Negotiation", *Journal of Personality and Social Psychology* 91, No. 4 (2005): 493–512.

8.2 TEAM NEGOTIATIONS

A few years ago, I was working with a leading multinational where I was in charge of Procurement for Europe. We had to make some fairly large capital purchases, and for this project, I had to work with Engineering colleagues from another region I had never met or worked with.

Ahead of the negotiation, I prepared a detailed negotiation preparation template. One of those comprehensive templates featuring 55 different questions, so that we could explore all kinds of elements and avoid misalignment. Once I prepared this document, I sent it to my Engineering colleagues to get their point of view.

I sent it once, no reply. Sent it again, no reply. I then tried to reach them by phone, but they were traveling all the time, very busy, and impossible to get hold of. This happened a few years ago, when the means of communication was less sophisticated than those we have today.

Finally, we found a solution to align: 'We are meeting the supplier at 10:00am. Let's meet at 9:00am, then we have one hour together so that we can go through the different elements and make sure that we are really aligned for this negotiation.' My colleagues were supposed to arrive at 9:00, but due to an issue they only arrived 10 minutes before the start of the meeting. The supplier was already in the reception waiting for the meeting, so we ended up starting the meeting with no alignment.

After the introductory phase of the meeting, one of my two Engineering colleagues said to the supplier: 'I want you to be aware that we have chosen your technology for this project and we have a budget of 12 million dollars. Let's see how we can get the most from it.' All my negotiation strategies and preparation were completely wasted just a few minutes into the negotiation. I was so caught by surprise that I could not even come up with some mitigation statements, such as '12 million is the budget for the whole *category*, not only for this project!' or 'As you were travelling, you may have missed some of the latest changes on this project'.

Let's capture three learnings about team negotiations from my experience:

1. **Take time to align with your colleagues**. Ideally, you should prepare the negotiation together and start the alignment process well ahead of the negotiation. This allows the parties to align with their respective bosses and perhaps explore other creative ideas.

2. **Give roles to each meeting participant**. This ensures that participants in the negotiation know what they have to do. For instance, it is important to clarify upfront who is going to be the lead negotiator and who will be the decision-maker. You can then go on to identify all different kinds of roles, such as technical, commercial, number-cruncher, note-taker, body language observer, questioner, proposal-maker, and good or bad guy. When negotiation participants know their role, they can participate more effectively during the meeting, and they are more motivated.

3. **Call a caucus to realign**. During the negotiation, some new elements may come up that you had not planned in advance, or perhaps you are confronted with unexpected behaviour. By calling a break, you can get together with

your team, discuss any new evidence and go back to the negotiation table once you are again on the same page.

8.3 PREPARING FOR CROSS-CULTURAL NEGOTIATIONS

I wrote this paragraph in my hotel room in Riyadh, Saudi Arabia, after completing a negotiation with a local company. The differences with Italy, my country of origin, or Switzerland, the country where I have been living for over 25 years, are sharp. For instance, the approach to punctuality in meetings is completely different compared to Switzerland. This place inspired me to think about how to prepare for cross-cultural negotiations.

When we prepare for these negotiations, there is a tendency to focus only on the surface, looking at the kind of **etiquette elements** that may be part of the local culture. This may include how people greet each other, what kind of body language element should be considered, whether eye contact is polite, if there any gestures which are impolite or offensive, and if it a good idea or not to exchange gifts. Knowledge of these factors is indeed necessary because it will prevent big mistakes. At the same time, we could go deeper in our preliminary research.

Your preparation should also include any **economic or political factors** that may have an impact on your negotiation, and more importantly the **deeper cultural and process issues** that may give you some insight into the way the other culture negotiates.

Here are some questions that can help us reflect on these deeper issues:

- Is this more of a culture that focuses on the deal, like the Americans, or is it more of a culture where you have to build the relationship first, like the Chinese?
- Do they tend to have a long-term or short-term focus? For instance, I struggle to see in Europe the long-term focus that Japanese people may have.
- Is it a hierarchical or more egalitarian culture? When Renault and Volvo made a joint venture for trucks, they experienced a number of cross-cultural issues because of the differences between the more hierarchical French culture and the more egalitarian Swedish one. At the meetings, the French would send the Directors (because important meetings are managed by senior executives), while the Swedish would send the Managers (because they would know the details).

There are a number of researchers that tried to classify the key traits of a culture. A widely known classification is the one by the Dutch psychologist Geert Hofstede. You may find a description of his theory of cultural dimensions on the web, as well as the possibility to compare different countries over these dimensions.[3]

To conclude, I want to remind you that **a country of origin's culture is only one of the elements that shapes a person's behaviour.** Other factors that shape the way the other person behaves include company culture, functional culture (i.e. which role they had inside an organisation), gender, religion, and the countries where they lived. As a

---

3   The Culture Factor, *Country Comparison Tool*, https://www.hofstede-insights. com/country-comparison/ (accessed April 3, 2025).

result, do not expect everyone in one country to behave in the same way. You should therefore use the information about the country's culture as an initial hypothesis, then test this hypothesis during the negotiation.

8.4 MANAGING CROSS-CULTURAL TEAM NEGOTIATIONS

Will you soon be involved in cross-cultural negotiations?

Most likely some of your colleagues will also be part of the same negotiation. Here are three points to keep in mind that can help you to deal effectively with cross-cultural negotiations in teams.

1. **Team size**. How many people will be at the meeting? Will it be a one-to-one meeting, a small team or a large team? Consider also the habits in the country where you are going for the negotiation. If, for instance, you are dealing with a collectivistic culture, such as Japan or China, then they are likely to have a larger team rather than a small one. When feasible, I suggest having a comparably sized team to the one that you will expect from the counterpart. I also want you to know that research[4] indicates that teams who are having difficulties building trust with the other party achieve better results with one-to-one negotiations. If your aim is to build trust, you may want to have a few one-to-one meetings with your counterpart before you sit at the table with a larger team.

2. **Team composition**. Who should be at this meeting? Include one colleague from the country you are visiting, as they may help to bridge the cultural gap. If needed, bring your own translator. You want to make sure that the translator is on your side and can also help you to deal

---

4   J. T. Polzer, "Intergroup Negotiations," *Journal of Conflict Resolution* 40 (No. 4) (1996): 678–98.

with cultural differences. A personal friend and Chief Procurement Officer of a large chemical company shared an incident when he was about to turn down an invitation from an important Chinese supplier to go to a karaoke session. However, his translator helped him realise that the karaoke night was an important component of the trust-building process.

3. **Team alignment**. Make sure that you plan a substantial amount of time for team alignment and preparation. You may need to train negotiation participants on basic negotiation skills. You want to identify upfront the specific information that cannot be shared, and align your methodology to deal with team misalignments (calling a break, private chats via messaging applications, etc.). Given the other aspects of misalignment are bigger in cross-functional teams, we should therefore dedicate more time to the alignment process.

8.5 NONVERBAL COMMUNICATION

You may have learned in the past that certain postures or gestures are associated with certain attitudes. For instance, having an open posture may be a sign of trust, or having a closed posture may be a sign of defensiveness. Or maybe leaning forward is a sign of showing an interest. Now, those are stereotypes. The reality is much more complex. It is possible you may have a closed posture because it is comfortable for you, or maybe because it is cold. Therefore, **a single gesture or posture is not enough to draw conclusions regarding the attitude of a person in a negotiation**.

My advice in reading body language is to **look at a combination of elements in the context of the interaction**. Let me clarify this point.

When facing your counterpart during a negotiation, do not focus on only one element in the nonverbal communication. Instead, look for more signs during your interaction with them. Several years ago, I had just met a new colleague from Vietnam, and we ended up going for lunch together. At the lunch table, after five or ten minutes, I asked him: 'I am passionate about the history of Vietnam; can you please tell me what you think about...' and I gave him the name of a historical leader. As I asked him this question, I noticed that he shifted backwards in his chair, crossed his arms, and there was a long pause. Then, with a hesitant voice, he gave me a superficial answer. In this specific context of interaction, I could see a number of signs that gave me the message that the person was uncomfortable with the topic. In fact, it was not very smart of me to raise such a topic considering that I had only met the person for such a short time.

The other element you want to keep in mind is that there are also **cross-cultural differences in nonverbal communication**. Be careful in trying to read someone's body language while assuming your own cultural standards. In addition, it is a good idea to learn what kind of gesture may be offensive to certain cultures and recognise that we may have different paradigms. As an example, when negotiating with a counterpart from the south of India, you may have noticed that to say 'Yes' they move their heads in a lateral way, which is quite different from the vertical movement typical in the Western world.

Here is a personal example of failing to see cross-cultural differences in nonverbal communication. Several years ago, I was negotiating with a Chinese woman who did not make eye contact with me. My initial assumption, as a Westerner, is that a person who does not make eye contact may be untrustworthy. Luckily, I asked one of my former Chinese students to give her advice and she explained to me that in some regions of China, the children, especially the girls, are raised by their parents with the message, 'To be polite, do not make eye contact with someone who is older or more senior than you.' If this person follows their mother's advice as they grow up, they may not look at you directly during the negotiation in order to be polite.

8.6 DEALING WITH INTERNAL NEGOTIATIONS

As I hear from many of my workshop participants and as confirmed by leading negotiation experts,[5] internal negotiations are more challenging than external ones. So here are three points that can help you to deal more effectively with internal negotiations.

1. **Prepare for your internal negotiations**. We have often been told to prepare for external negotiations, while we fail to prepare for internal ones. Preparing for an internal negotiation using one of the traditional negotiation preparation tools may be helpful. In addition, you may also want to complete a stakeholder mapping exercise and a stakeholder analysis. The aim is to understand all the different parties who are involved in internal negotiations and then **capture the interests** of each person. For key decision meetings, you may also want to build a better idea about their values, beliefs, preferences, and personality types so that you know whom you are dealing with.

2. **Have a strategy to deal with conflicting interests**. Inevitably, as different departments are driven by different priorities, you will end up having misalignments and differences. A wise approach will be to speak openly about these. For instance, we know that Finance may be driven by profit, Procurement by cost savings, R&D by

5   H. Falcao, "Four Reasons Why Internal Negotiations Are Harder Than External Ones," *INSEAD Knowledge*, July 2017, https://knowledge.insead.edu/leadership-organisations/four-reasons-why-internal-negotiations-are-harder-external-ones, accessed April 3, 2025.

innovation, and Sales by volume. Communicating those differences and encouraging open sharing of available information will enable everyone to put their perspectives on the table. Then a decision can be made which considers all these key elements.

3. **Ensure alignment for next steps**. This may happen when a team goal is sponsored by top management, which provides guidance to everyone. An approach frequently used is agreeing to a scoring system to drive decisions. A scoring system is a tool that takes into account multiple dimensions that will be used in decision-making. For instance, let us say the team has to decide on the selected supplier for a project, from three contenders. The decision may be based 30% on cost, 30% on quality, 20% on innovation capabilities, 10% on Environmental, Social and Governance (ESG) standards and 10% on service. The next step is to decide which different elements inside of those five dimensions will drive our decision.

4. **Consider putting yourself in the CEO's shoes**. What would be the best outcome for the company overall? Building common ground as if you were the CEO drives consensus over what is best overall for the company vs. the individual functional objectives and it is often a bridge-builder in internal negotiations.

8.7 ETHICS AND NEGOTIATION

How do I find the right balance between being ethical and being effective in a negotiation?

Let's start by defining what we mean by ethics. My suggested definition is 'agreed principles about what is right and what is wrong'. The challenge is that what is right or wrong may change depending on the context, the personality of the negotiators, and their culture.

To illustrate this idea, let me share with you a brief research that I did a few years ago. I asked several people of different genders, age groups, and nationalities how they would act in the following situation: 'You are going to a shop and the cashier gives you more money than is appropriate. What will you do?'. Some people replied to me, 'Well, I will give the money back right away.' Other people said, 'Well, it really depends. Maybe if it is a small shop, then I will give the money back. But if it is a big supermarket, then I will just keep it.' Somebody else said, 'Well, I will keep the money because this type of mistake happens in both directions. Whenever it is against me, I lose it. Therefore, whenever it is *for* me, I have to keep it. And then it will be even over time.'

You can see that in the same type of context, **different people believe themselves to be ethical even though they behave in substantially different ways**.

When we look at ethics in negotiation, certain individuals believe that hiding information or displaying fake emotions, like pretending to be angry, is considered unethical, while for others it is perfectly normal and simply a part of the negotiation game.

Here is another example of differing standards. Some negotiators say: 'I do not lie and I do not mislead' because this is the best way to build trust in the long term; others say, 'I do not lie but I am OK with misleading, because this will improve my negotiation outcome'; still others say, 'I am OK with lying and misleading, because these are some of the tools that are available in negotiation to reach my goals and defend the interests of my company!'. What option should I choose? How do we find the balance between ethics and effectiveness in negotiation? Can I be effective in negotiation by being fully ethical, open and transparent, even when I am in a weak situation such as having no alternatives?

Decisions around ethics are very personal and we are not here to decide the standards that one should follow, although in the long term it is beneficial to be perceived as a trustworthy person (see 3.8). As we talked with several experienced negotiators about the standards they used, we received the following advice that may offer a few possible paths to consider for your own standards.

1. 'Do not lie, but use the truth to your advantage.' This is about presenting the information in the way that is more effective to you.
2. When going into a negotiation, you cannot be too open and transparent. To feel better with yourself, imagine it is your 'alter-ego' who is going to the negotiation or imagine that you are 'putting on your negotiation jacket'.
3. Look for strategies that may help you to avoid lying in negotiations, such as preparing in advance some of the difficult questions you will most likely be asked. Not answering some of the questions, or proposing to answer

a different question. Let's imagine that you are in a salary negotiation with a potential employer, and they ask you 'What is your current salary?'. Unfortunatcly, your current salary is very low, and this may prevent you from receiving the compensation you want in the new job. In such a situation, you may still reply to a different question, such as: 'I do not want to talk about my current salary because it applies to a different industry and function; however, you should know that I am currently targeting jobs with a compensation range between X and Y thousand euros.'

4. Adapt your approach to the context. Your attitude will differ if you are buying something one-off at a street market or if you are negotiating with a long-term partner.

8.8 CREATIVITY IN NEGOTIATION

Is creativity important in negotiations? Absolutely!

Using creativity in negotiations provides a number of benefits, such as:

- **Offering choices to your counterparts**. When presented with alternative proposals, people may compare these to each other instead of to their original goals. When making a proposal to your counterpart, think ahead about other options that you could offer that meet your interests (see section 9.5 for more information about making Multiple Equivalent Simultaneous Offers).
- **Determining interests of other parties**. Creativity can open doors by making individuals realise their real interests. During the preparation phase, you should have estimated the interests and priorities of your counterpart. You can then brainstorm possible proposals that could meet their interests.
- **Creating value for both parties.** Creativity can transform a fight over price or a deadlock into a win–win agreement. For instance, when the two parties are positioning around price, a possible way to move forward is to make concessions. Often, a more effective way is to bring value-added elements that can be beneficial to one or both parties.

Here are four effective strategies to increase creativity in your negotiations:

1. **Create a trust-based climate**. When there is trust with your counterpart, there is willingness to share information and openness to exploring different ideas.
2. **Use incubation to generate new ideas**. This is about giving yourself time to come up with ideas, so rather than trying to solve all the negotiation problems right away, give yourself one hour, one day, or one week so that you can come up with better and more creative ideas.
3. **In addition to playing with the existing negotiation variables, consider adding new variables or new topics to your agreement**. For instance, adding a clause that takes into account the economic outlook may reassure one of the parties to go for a longer-term agreement.
4. **Focus your creativity on satisfying the most important interests**. Identify the key interests and priorities for you and your counterpart(s), then identify a number of different ways to satisfy the interests of both parties.

8.9 NEGOTIATING WITH FAMILY AND FRIENDS

Perhaps you never do business with friends or family, but chances are you will have to negotiate at one time or another over significant financial, business, or investment decisions with someone you care for.

Those situations present a different set of challenges than standard negotiations. Negotiations with family and friends are often more complex and challenging than those involving unrelated individuals. The longstanding nature of family relationships fosters deeply ingrained dynamics, some of which can support constructive negotiations, others of which may pose obstacles.

According to Harvard Professors Deepak Malhotra and John Davis,[6] a pre-existing close relationship among friends or partners is more likely to lead to a mutually acceptable outcome in negotiation than between two complete strangers. This may be due to trust, a greater openness to communication, information sharing, and both sides' desire to expand the pie rather than divide it. A typical strength of family negotiations is that family members generally prefer to reach mutually acceptable outcomes in their negotiations due to their close ties, which can facilitate cooperation and reduce dysfunctional competition.

However, the closeness between the parties can lead to less effective negotiation outcomes as parties may avoid expressing their true interests to maintain the relationship.

---

6   D. Malhotra and J.A. Davis, "Five Steps to Better Family Negotiations," *HBS Working Knowledge*, July 9, 2007, https://www.library.hbs.edu/working-knowledge/five-steps-to-better-family-negotiations (accessed April 3 2025).

As a result, they are often not as successful in overall value creation as compared to negotiating with strangers.

Here are four strategies that may help you when faced with these situations:

1. **Preserve the relationship**. When negotiating with family and friends, relationships are very important. As a result, you may apply the same approach that you use when negotiating in long-term business relationships. With friends or family, you may even be more committed to a win–win solution, because you are operating under a sort of 'generosity norm'. This can also cause you to act outside of your own best interest. Therefore, there are two options. Ideally, listen, explore ideas and take time to discuss, with an open communication so that not only there is a good relationship, but also a strong outcome. The second option is that in order to preserve the relationship, there is a possibility for a suboptimal outcome because the relationship is so important to you.

2. **Generate positive emotions**. Whenever we are negotiating with family and friends, emotions tend to get in the way. When I communicate with business executives and I ask them, 'What is your advice on dealing with emotions?', the reply that I get more often than not is simply, 'Do not get emotional in negotiation.' Well, guess what? This is unlikely to happen, because emotions exist. So rather than suppressing emotions during negotiations with family and friends, focus on generating positive emotions while interacting with them.

There are a number of techniques to generate positive emotion. Let me stress one of them that I discovered over 10 years ago from a wonderful book by John Gottman, *Why Marriages Succeed or Fail*. I recommend reading this book, especially if you are a newlywed. In this book, John Gottman describes some research that he and his team have done to try and predict whether a couple will stay together or go through a divorce. And they are able to predict this with 95% accuracy. Their approach is based on studying the newlywed couple, and how they have handled a recent conflict. They have observation cameras in the room to monitor what happens during the exchange, including some that look at micro-facial expressions of emotions. The key predictor about whether the couple will stay together or not is whether they are able to **communicate their appreciation for each other** and their ability to convey positive emotions. According to Gottman, the ratio between the positive messages and the negative messages is on average five to one for the couples that stay together, while on average only one to one for the couples that will end up going through divorce.

Now, if we know that appreciation is important, how do we bring about appreciation in a negotiation? The first way to do this is by active listening, making sure that we really pay attention and genuinely understand what is being said. The second way to show appreciation is to look for positives: anything that they do well, think well, and express well.

3. **Make a conscious effort to encourage sharing interests**. Those in close relationships often refrain from expressing their own interests and priorities, even on

matters of great importance, opting instead to compromise broadly to avoid being seen as selfish or overly self-focused. Fear of conflict can lead couples to avoid putting their own interests forward in order not to damage the relationship, which prevents maximising value creation. As a result, it becomes essential for family members and friends to actively encourage one another to express their interests and concerns. If you are the kind of person who is uncomfortable with any degree of conflict, perhaps you should reframe it as problem-solving and use some of the value creation ideas we expressed in Chapter 4.

4. **Bring a third party.** If one of the parties is unwilling to share interests or approach the discussion with a win–win attitude, then we may consider bringing a third party, like a mediator.

Ultimately, candour will be your best tool in dealing with friends or family members. Discuss what your interests are, heed their positions too, and work toward a mutually beneficial solution. It may turn out to be a more pleasant negotiation than you would think.

8.10 ENSURING A RESPONSE TO YOUR QUESTIONS IN A NEGOTIATION

How can you increase the chances to receive a reply to your questions during a negotiation?

We know this is not an easy task, because most of the people are reluctant to share information during the negotiation process as they are afraid that this may be used against them. This is part of the negotiator's dilemma of finding a balance between cooperation and competition.

Here are six tips that can increase your chances of getting a reply to your questions.

1. **Create a climate of trust**. When there is a good relationship between the parties, the other party will feel more comfortable sharing information.
2. **Start with easy questions**. Those are the kind of questions that do not put your counterpart at a disadvantage.
3. **Formulate your questions in a neutral way**. A neutral question may be: 'How is the project going?'. A biased request may be: 'Help me understand why we are running behind and why there are so many problems on this project.'
4. **Be prepared to share information**. This ensures that you can reciprocally build understanding, and you are perceived as a fair counterpart.
5. **Provide an explanation before asking the question**. If you only ask questions, the negotiation may sound like a police interrogation: 'Why did you do this? Why do you want that?'. It is therefore better to give an explanation before you question: 'I am keen to understand more about

your interest in strengthening the collaboration with us. What is behind this request to sign a three-year contract?'.

6. **Pre-empt a difficult question**. You may say something like, 'I do understand that this is sensitive information, so can you share more insights about your R&D pipeline?'.

8.11 HOW TO GET OUT OF A DEADLOCK

It is indeed a powerful negotiation technique to enter into a deadlock, maybe to signal that the proposal from the other party is unacceptable. On the other hand, we also want to find a solution to get out of a deadlock.

Here are eight ways that can help you escape from a deadlock in a negotiation.

1. **Call for a break**. Taking a timeout will enable the intense emotions to calm down and prevent an escalation or a full stop to the negotiations. You can then still find a solution when emotions are less intense.
2. **Share some additional information**. By giving an explanation, you open up new ways to look for a solution.
3. **Offer a small concession**. This will signal collaboration. (You can then ask something else in return.)
4. **Highlight the negative consequences of not reaching an agreement**. Then reframe the collaboration in more positive and collaborative terms.
5. **Think outside the box and look for new options to move forward**. Sometimes adding a new element into the negotiation may enable us to find a solution, while we are unable to find one with the current elements.
6. **Change the setting**. Just changing the location may be a powerful tool to recalibrate. Rather than having the meeting in one of the two parties' premises, consider taking the meeting to a restaurant to create a neutral, more positive type of environment. Another option is to move from a virtual to a face-to-face meeting.

7. **Change the negotiation team**. Usually it is about escalating, going one level up. At times, the people at the lower level in the organisation may not have the authority to come up with new options.

8. **Involve a third party**. This does not happen very often in a business context, but it tends to happen much more in diplomacy or in private matters, such as involving a mediator to solve disputes between a couple.

8.12 CHAPTER 8 IN A NUTSHELL

Negotiate the process before you negotiate the substance. Ask a number of questions to ensure that you are clear on how you will negotiate.

Three key points to keep in mind for effective team negotiations:

- Take time to align with your colleagues, ideally preparing the negotiation together in writing
- Give roles to each meeting participant
- Call a caucus to realign when confronted with new evidence.

To prepare for cross-cultural negotiations be aware about:

- Etiquette elements
- Economic and political factors that may impact the negotiations
- Deeper cultural and process factors that are specific to that culture
- In addition, remember that the country's culture is only one of the many elements that shapes the behaviour of one individual.

Three considerations that can help you to manage cross-cultural negotiations in teams:

- Decide the right team size
- Define who should be at the meeting

- Plan a larger than usual amount of time to strengthen team alignment.

When trying to read the nonverbal communication of your counterpart, consider multiple elements in the context of interaction and pay attention to cross-cultural differences.

Here are the four strategies to be effective in internal negotiations:

- Prepare for your internal negotiation, including mapping your stakeholders
- Know how to deal with conflicting interests among different departments
- Develop the right tools to ensure alignment for future decisions
- Consider putting yourself in the CEO's shoes.

Regarding ethics and negotiation, you may take into account the following:

- There is no universal standard on what is considered to be ethical in negotiations
- Decisions and choices around ethics are very personal
- We provided a few possible options on how to deal with ethics and negotiation so that you can make your own choices.

To increase creativity in your negotiation:

- Create a trust-based climate to encourage information sharing
- Use incubation to generate new ideas
- Consider adding new topics or variables to your negotiation strategy
- Focus your creativity on satisfying the most important interests.

A few key ideas to negotiate with family and friends:

- Preserve the relationship
- Approach the discussion with a win-win spirit
- Eventually accept a suboptimal outcome to preserve the relationship
- Generate positive emotions. (One way of doing this is to focus on appreciation)
- Make sure that both parties share interests and priorities with each other
- Bring a third party if one of the parties is not willing to collaborate.

Six ideas to ensure you receive a response to your question:

- Create a climate of trust
- Start with easy questions
- Formulate your questions as neutrally as possible
- Be prepared to share information
- Give an explanation before formulating your questions

- Inform the other party upfront ahead of a difficult question being asked.

Eight ways that can help you get out of a deadlock:

- Call for a break
- Share some additional information
- Offer a small concession
- Highlight the negative consequences of not reaching an agreement
- Think outside the box and look for new options to move forward
- Change the setting
- Change the negotiation team
- Involve a third party.

CHAPTER 9

ADVANCED NEGOTIATION

9.1 PREVENTING PEOPLE FROM LYING TO YOU

How can you prevent people from lying to you?

You can never fully prevent people from lying to you, although there are a few techniques that can help. Here are four ways, some inspired by Max Bazerman and Deepak Malhotra, authors of the excellent book *Negotiation Genius*,[1] that can certainly reduce the likelihood that people will lie to you.

1. **Look prepared**. Once you have a discussion with someone, state references to previous discussions (for instance, by mentioning the date of your previous meeting), show that you are able to discuss details, and provide comments based on the notes that you have taken. When you are well prepared, the negotiating party

---

1   D. Malhotra and M. Bazerman. 2007. *Negotiation Genius*. Harvard Business School.

is less likely to lie to you because they are afraid that you may spot the lie.

2. **Signal your ability to obtain information**. Imagine you are interviewing a candidate, and you are afraid that they may lie about their current salary. You may then say, 'We interviewed a number of people from your company and already have a pretty good idea about the compensation levels. Still, can you please tell me what your exact compensation is today?'.

3. **Do not lie**. Sometimes people lie out of self-defence because they believe that you are lying to them. If you give them some evidence that you told the truth in the past, or if you are sharing some information that can make you vulnerable, then you are more likely to create a trust-based relationship without lies.

4. **Build relationships**. Negotiators are less likely to lie to someone with whom they have a good relationship.

We also know that men are more likely to be dishonest, particularly when rewards are involved.[2] Pressures on negotiators (e.g. financial results) as well as being unprepared increase people's tendency to lie.

---

2   A. M. Garcia et al., "Gender Differences in Individual Dishonesty Profiles," *Frontiers in Psychology* 12 (December 2021), https://www.frontiersin.org/journals/psychology/articles/10.3389/fpsyg.2021.728115/full, accessed April 3, 2025.

9.2 NEGOTIATING A LONG-TERM AGREEMENT

Negotiating a long-term agreement is a complex matter. Here are some strategies you can apply in your negotiations that are applicable to all circumstances:

1. **Take time to build a relationship**. I assume that if you want to get married, you are not going to marry someone that you just met, even if he or she appears very attractive at first glance. Although it is less critical, even in business relationships you don't just leap into an agreement; that's because it is important to take time to build a relationship. Before the business negotiation, have a genuine conversation that is more than just a few minutes of small talk. Taking the time to build the relationship is particularly important if you are engaging in negotiation outside of the Western world, because many cultures value relationship-building as a prerequisite to a business relationship.

2. **Be trustworthy**. When I talk about being trustworthy, I mean displaying ethical behaviour in your negotiation tactics. It means keeping promises while avoiding manipulation and lies.

3. **Make sure that you negotiate a deal where both parties are satisfied**. Especially when you have more power in a negotiation, you may be tempted to negotiate *too* good a deal. But unfortunately, when you push too much in your favour, this might compromise the sustainability of the deal. Here's an example from a few years ago, when I was a Procurement Director, negotiating with one of our IT outsourcing providers. The

outsourcing agreement had been made a few years prior, and it was up for renewal. Since the sourcing process had not been properly managed, we ended up being in a situation where we were locked with this supplier. We could neither use other suppliers, nor restart the work ourselves. As we prepared for the negotiations and did some benchmarking, we realised that our rates were substantially higher than the market. During the negotiation, we asked the supplier to align their rates with the market conditions but were confronted with an unwillingness to change the terms. Because of the challenging balance of power, at the end of the negotiation we ended up having to accept their terms with some minor modifications. However, such an approach did not create the conditions for a sustainable long-term agreement. At the end of the negotiation, we started to build an alternative so that we could work with someone else at the end of the contract terms, which we did two years later.

9.3 MULTIPARTY NEGOTIATIONS

In external negotiations, dealing with one counterpart is more common, and we are used to one-on-one strategies to reach an agreement with this counterpart. On the other hand, there will be situations when the complexity is higher and there are multiple parties involved.

For instance, let's take the example of an internal negotiation. You may be part of an executive committee, and you want the committee to make a decision that is important to you. Then what are you going to do to influence the other parties so that your views are retained?

Here are three strategies that will be useful in managing multiparty negotiations.

The first involves **identifying all key stakeholders**, which means the people sitting at the table, as well as the other people that influence the people at the table, and those who will have to be involved, directly or indirectly, during the decision process. And when you identify all the key individuals, then it is important to understand their interests and priorities. For instance, through this analysis, you will have a clearer picture about the individuals who will be in your favour, those who have doubts, and those that are more likely to oppose your idea.

The second is **to look at the right sequence to approach people**. In a multiparty negotiation, rather than waiting for the big meeting to take place, it is ideal to approach the key individuals prior to the negotiation to influence their decision. Based on the findings from your stakeholder mapping, decide who you are going to approach first and which topics you will discuss with each person. In this respect, it is often a good idea to start with the people that are in doubt, then aim to secure their commitment to support you.

The final piece of advice is to **define a decision process that supports your decision**. The decision may be based on consensus or democracy. It may be a public vote or secret vote. By choosing the decision process that works best in your favour, based on your analysis, then you can increase your chances of getting the outcome you want.

9.4 MANAGING INTERNAL AND EXTERNAL NEGOTIATIONS

Do you usually start with internal or external negotiations?

Most of the time, the best approach is to start with internal negotiations. An effective internal negotiation will give you a broader scope to create value in the external negotiation. In fact, your ability to negotiate effectively externally is strongly correlated with the quality of your internal negotiations.

To deal with internal negotiations well, I have three suggestions for you:

1. **Involve a diverse group of people in the preparation phase**. This will enable you to understand well what represents value for the company. In addition, sometimes people may block the deal just because they were not consulted. I am not advocating bringing many people to the negotiation table, as this may create further problems. Still, there is significant value in involving several internal stakeholders in the preparation.
2. **Understand hidden agendas**. I recall a real-life situation when R&D was working on a new development and was trying to block the introduction of a product from a supplier that seemed superior to their own product.
3. **Manage expectations**. Avoid entering into the negotiation with an expectation to decrease prices by 20% while the market is going up 10%. If stakeholders have unrealistic expectations, such as asking to have it cheap, fast and high quality, ask them to rank their priorities so that you have a better understanding about what is important.

The best negotiators do not focus only on their internal side, but also on the internal side of their counterpart. Three ways to do this well include:

- **Research the company and their country's culture**. You need to have a good understanding of how your counterpart operates.
- **Discover the internal dynamics of the other party**. This is best done before the negotiation, when their guard is down. You can then find allies that can help you to move the project forward (e.g. salespeople identify end-users and get them to use the product before the negotiation).
- **Prepare their victory speech**. Your counterpart will be scrutinised and judged by their bosses and their stakeholders. What would enable your counterpart to present the agreement as a victory to their stakeholders? If we are able to write your counterpart's victory speech, then we have a path to selling them the deal.

9.5 MULTIPLE EQUIVALENT SIMULTANEOUS OFFERS (MESOS)

Time to step out of your comfort zone!

Previous examples in this book have centred around exchanging one proposal. The technique we want to cover in this paragraph is called MESO, **Multiple Equivalent Simultaneous Offers**. In this format, you develop multiple offers that have the same or a similar value to you, then offer them simultaneously to your counterpart and ask them to choose one. This technique has a number of benefits versus the traditional single offer, because it signals flexibility. You provide a range of proposals, and your counterpart gets many options to choose from. It also gives you the opportunity to collect vital information, because as the other party explains which of the offers they prefer and why, you will understand their concerns and needs.

The MESO is effective also with certain individuals who don't seem interested in collaborating, as it helps you to gain a better understanding of their requirements. Another important benefit is that it enables you to anchor your deal (see 5.1). Instead of making one aggressive offer, you can now make *three* aggressive offers. Your anchoring effect will be stronger, and you will appear more flexible because of the three offers.

To create these multiple equivalent simultaneous offers, there are three key steps that you want to keep in mind.

1. **Identify the variables that you want to change**. If in a deal you have five or six variables or negotiable items, then you decide which are the two or three that will stay stable during each of the proposals, and which are the

ones that will change among the proposals. You should usually have three variables that will change from one offer to another to provide variations and choices.

2. **Understand the value of those variables**. In order to prepare three offers that are of the same value to you, it is important to be clear about the value of each variable to you, ideally using a scoring system[3] that enables you to compare different issues. As an example, if you change the intellectual property, or if you change the payment terms, or if you change the contract length, then you should be clear on the value of each factor to you so that you can make equivalent offers.

3. **Create three offers of equivalent value and ask the other party which one they prefer**. Research from Northwestern University[4] shows that the best thing to do is indeed to have three offers, because making more than that unnecessarily increases the complexity. Then get the other party to choose their preferred one. Even if they do not like any of the three, ask them which one they would prefer, so that you have an indication about which direction you can move this forward.

Let me give a simplified example of how multiple simultaneous equivalent offers may look. Usually, you would change more than two parameters, but let's make this simple and just

---

3   D. Ames, R. Larrick and M. Morris, "Scoring a deal: Valuing outcomes in multi-issue negotiations," *Columbia CaseWorks* (March 5, 2012), https://www.columbia.edu/~ms4992/negotiations/Scoring%20a%20Deal.pdf, accessed 3 April 2025.

4   G. Leonardelli et al, "Multiple Equivalent Simultaneous Offers (MESOs) Reduce the Negotiator Dilemma: How a Choice of First Offers Increases Economic and Relational Outcomes," *Organizational Behavior and Human Decision Processes* 152 (May 2005), 64–83.

stick with two: Suppose you are a salesman, then your offer will be, 'Well, if you give me a hundred and fifty tonnes of product, I can accept your payment terms of 90 days. If you give me a hundred and twenty-five tonnes of product, then we can go for payment terms of 60 days. If you only give me a hundred tonnes, then we have to stay with the payment terms of 30 days.'

9.6 EMOTIONAL INTELLIGENCE AND NEGOTIATION

In this paragraph, we want to talk about the link between emotional intelligence and negotiation. There are many benefits of emotional intelligence. In particular, we can imagine that high emotional intelligence increases the possibility for a negotiator to build trust with the other person and to establish a productive long-term relationship. Something we are less familiar with is the fact that at times high emotional intelligence—in particular high empathy—may result in a negative effect on negotiations. This can include giving excessive concessions, even before the negotiation has started. Here's an example from my professional experience.

I was preparing with a colleague ahead of a supplier negotiation and the colleague with higher empathy said, 'Well, the company we are dealing with is a small company. They may not have the capabilities to deliver the project in 16 weeks. Let's ask for 18 weeks.' If you do this and you ask for 18 weeks, guess what is likely to happen during the meeting? The supplier says, 'Well, 18 weeks is too tight. Can we make it in 20 weeks?'.

In negotiation, empathy may be less effective than perspective-taking. Let me clarify the difference between the two. Empathy is about imagining **how the other party may feel**. Perspective-taking is imagining **how the other party may think**. So as much as empathy is an effective means of increasing the satisfaction of the other party, perspective-taking is more effective in delivering superior results for you. Research in 2008 by Professor Adam Galinsky,[5] who is now at Columbia Business School, indicated that as much as emotional intelligence and empathy are valuable social skills across several aspects of life, in negotiation, perspective-taking is a more effective skill. Perspective-taking increased individuals' ability to discover hidden agreements and to both create and claim value at the bargaining table.

Building on the results of this research and taking into account my practical experience, there are two key messages I want you to retain:

1. **Be emotionally aware, but not emotionally invested**. Leverage your ability to recognise your own and other people's emotions, without getting carried away by the concern for the counterpart.
2. Recognising that perspective-taking may be difficult to do in practice since we are too invested in our own head, consider the option of '**perspective-getting**'. This means approaching the negotiation by asking questions and a real willingness to understand the other side.

---

5   A.D. Galinski et al, "Why It Pays to Get Inside the Head of Your Opponent: The Differential Effects of Perspective Taking and Empathy in Negotiations," *Psychological Science* 19, no. 4 (2008), 378-84.

9.7 HOW LARGE LANGUAGE MODELS ARE REVOLUTIONISING NEGOTIATION

This is the last paragraph I wrote for this book and most likely the one that will become obsolete first.

Negotiation is often viewed as a deeply human skill—an art that blends empathy, persuasion, and strategy. But what happens when cutting-edge AI, particularly Large Language Models (LLMs), steps into the room? These advanced tools, like OpenAI's ChatGPT, Claude, Gemini, etc., are transforming the way professionals prepare for and approach negotiations.

In this paragraph, we will explore how LLMs are reshaping the negotiation landscape and how you can leverage them today to gain a competitive edge, recognising that the landscape is changing very quickly.

Large language models are sophisticated AI systems trained on vast amounts of text data. They excel at understanding context, generating coherent responses, and even predicting conversational dynamics. Here's how they're becoming invaluable in negotiation scenarios:

1. **Enhanced preparation**

Preparation is the backbone of successful negotiation. LLMs can:

*   **Analyse key information**: Summarise contracts, reports, or past data to assist negotiators in identifying critical points.

- **Research counterparts**: Provide insights into an organisation's history, priorities, and industry trends, allowing you to anticipate their needs. Using AI-based personality tools, such as Humantic.ai or Crystalknows.com, you can identify the counterpart's communication and negotiation styles and preferences.
- **Develop scenarios**: Give a description of the negotiation, being specific about your interests and priorities. Then you can ask for advice on a number of topics, such as: What would be the right negotiation strategy, what questions to ask, what questions you are likely to get from your counterpart, what arguments to use, etc. This will enable you to rehearse and refine your strategy.

2. Real-time support

While negotiation unfolds, LLMs can serve as a discreet assistant:

- **On-demand insights**: Quickly retrieve facts, numbers, or definitions to clarify points during discussions.
- **Reframe arguments**: Suggest alternative phrasing for proposals or rebuttals to maintain a collaborative tone.
- **Provide real-time coaching**: Overcome impasse or deadlock or shift strategy when new information becomes available, by feeding the LLM with a real-time transcript of the negotiations.
- **Language translation**: Break down barriers in international negotiations with a real-time translation support.

3. **Data-driven decision-making**

Negotiation involves making complex decisions under pressure. LLMs can process vast amounts of data to:

- Identify patterns or trends that inform decision-making
- Highlight potential risks and rewards of various options
- Help you evaluate offers with clarity and confidence.

It's essential to recognise that **LLMs are tools—not substitutes for human judgment**. Negotiation is as much about emotional intelligence as it is about data. LLMs can enhance your capabilities, but building trust, reading body language, and understanding unspoken nuances remain uniquely human strengths. By combining the analytical power of LLMs with a collaborative mindset, negotiators can:

- Save time on preparation
- Approach discussions with increased confidence
- Create more value for all parties involved.

Conclusion: The future of negotiation is here, and it's powered by AI. By embracing tools like large language models and AI agents, you can prepare smarter, negotiate better, and achieve outcomes that benefit everyone at the table, as the recent study *When AI Joins the Table*, from my friend and colleague Yadvinder Rana, indicates.[6]

---

6   Y.S. Rana, "When AI Joins the Table: How Large Language Models Transform Negotiations," *SSRN* (December 9, 2024).

9.8 CHAPTER 9 IN A NUTSHELL

To reduce the likelihood that someone is lying to you:

- Look prepared
- Signal your ability to obtain information
- Do not lie
- Build relationships.

Three key strategies to negotiate a long-term agreement:

- Take time to build a relationship
- Be trustworthy
- Make sure that you have an agreement where both parties are satisfied.

Some techniques to keep in mind when involved in multi-party negotiations:

- Identify all of the key stakeholders that are involved in the decision
- Decide the right sequence to approach different people outside of the negotiating table
- Recommend a decision process that favours your decision.

When managing internal and external negotiations:

- Start with internal negotiations
- Involve several people in the preparation phase, while understanding their hidden agendas and carefully managing their expectations

- Consider how you can help your counterpart to sell the deal to their own stakeholders, such as writing their victory speech.

Three key steps that you want to keep in mind when creating multiple equivalent simultaneous offers:

- Identify the variables that you want to change
- Understand the value of each of those variables
- Create three offers of equivalent value to you, then ask the other party which one they prefer.

To understand the link between emotional intelligence and negotiation:

- Emotional intelligence is a powerful tool to build stronger relationships while increasing the satisfaction of the other party
- Perspective-taking, i.e. imagining how the other party may think, is more effective than empathy at the negotiation table to create and claim value
- Be emotionally aware, but not emotionally invested
- Perspective-getting, i.e. asking questions and aiming to understand the other party, is a simpler alternative to perspective-taking.

Large Language Models are having a huge impact on negotiation. Already today, they can help us to:

- Improve preparation
- Provide real-time support

- Support data-driven decision-making.

It is key that negotiators start embracing AI tools such as Large Language Models and AI agents.

CHAPTER 10

CAREER MATTERS

10.1 HOW TO GET A RAISE – KNOWING YOUR WORTH

Do you find it difficult to ask your boss for a raise?

This is common to many professionals. Being well prepared can certainly increase your confidence. One of the key elements of your preparation is **understanding your market value**. You have to do your research both externally and internally.

When you want to understand your market value, you may immediately think about **websites like Glassdoor or PayScale** that share information about how much you may be earning when working at other companies. And of course that is a good starting point, but it should be only one of the elements of your data research.

Another piece of information comes from reaching out to **head-hunters** and getting their perspective about your market value. In a similar fashion, you should also be checking the **market reports** published by recruiting firms and surveys made by professional associations in your specific job function to better understand the typical compensation in the same field as yours.

Another often-neglected resource that is very powerful is **obtaining salary information from your network**. The good news is that we know a lot of people. The challenge is that most of the people do not like to talk about their salary. So how does one get salary information from people without making them feel uncomfortable? The key advice is, do not ask about their salary, but about your own salary instead. The way you ask the question to your network could be: 'I am exploring other job opportunities in my area of expertise in this region. Based on your experience and knowledge of the job market, considering that I have X years of experience, have this diploma and worked at these companies, what would be the right compensation range for me?'.

As you speak to a variety of different people and you complement it with your research online, then you will have a clearer picture about the right compensation range outside of your company.

The other element of preparation is to **understand how well you are paid inside your own company**. Now for certain companies, this is easy because the salary bands are disclosed to employees. But for many other companies, the salary information is not public knowledge, and you need to do some detective work. You may be tempted to say, 'I am going to do a quick benchmark with my good friends. We are doing the same job. And then I will have an idea whether I am paid well or less well.' That is a bad idea, because when you start benchmarking with your close colleagues and then you discover that someone is making 15% more or less than you, guess what? The relationship between the two colleagues is not going to be the same again, as this will create tension at work.

It is more effective to do such **benchmarking with people that have already left the company**, or one can get this **information from a senior sponsor** inside the company that can give you an insight into how well you are being compensated compared to a broad range of people.

10.2 HOW TO GET A RAISE – MAKING THE REQUEST

Do you know how to ask your boss for a raise?

Something that you are probably going to do as part of your preparation is preparing a longer list of achievements of all the things that you have done in order to justify your raise. Let me share with you a few more ideas.

The first piece of advice is **do not make your list of achievements too long**; just focus on your key achievements because to influence quality is more important than quantity. A few strong achievements are better than giving a long list of less impressive ones. When you make a long list of achievements, you may be challenged on the weakest ones, which will weaken your overall argument.

When you prepare the list of high-quality achievements, **remember to include the most important ones in first and last place**. This is because of the two psychological effects of primacy and recency,[1] which indicates that the most powerful effects are from the arguments which come first (primacy) and last (recency). If we go even more in depth then we know that the primacy effect lasts for a longer period, while the recency effect stays in people's minds during the moment itself. So, if the person is going to make a decision at that moment, then put your strongest argument last. Alternatively, if the person is going to make the decision later (which is usually the case for a request for a raise in larger companies), then take advantage of the primacy effect by putting your strongest achievement first.

---

1   N. Kolenda, *Methods of Persuasion* (Kindle Edition, 2013).

Once you have made your list of achievements, then you are going to **make a specific request**: 'I believe these achievements deserve a raise, so I wanted to ask you to give me a 12% raise as of the first of November.' Using an unrounded number like 12% is beneficial, because it sounds more researched and professional. Also mention a timeline, because you do not want this process to drag for too long.

Another point to note is that when you make this request, make sure it is **a bit higher than the number that you really want**. By mentioning a specific number or percentage, you take advantage of a psychological effect of anchoring. At the same time, your anchor should be more aggressive than what you really want so that you have some room for negotiation, while remaining reasonable.

10.3 HOW TO GET A RAISE – DEALING WITH A NEGATIVE REPLY

Is it easy to get a yes when you ask your boss for a raise?

For many professionals, unfortunately the answer is no. In fact, even if you have done a very good job, there may be reasons why you will not get a raise (e.g. the company is going through a difficult time, there may be no budget, you are already at the top of the salary band and there is no space for a promotion). How do you deal with a negative response?

The key advice in this area is to **identify a list of 'yes-able' alternatives**. Before a decision is taken regarding your request for a raise, you should be clear on what else would be valuable to you in case you cannot get one. In your preparation, you may consider four categories:

- Financial (e.g. bonus, stock options)
- Tangible (e.g. company car, insurance package)
- Intangible (e.g. job title, increased remote working)
- Job related (e.g. additional responsibilities, a plan to get a raise or a promotion).

So even if you get a negative reply in your request for a raise, you should suggest something else that your boss can do that you would highly appreciate. Your proposal will depend on your preferences and also on the rationale raised by your manager for not giving you a raise.

When making the request, **make sure to highlight 'What's in it for them'**. For instance, when I was negotiating with my employer to have more time for my teaching activity, rather than talking about my passion for teaching,

I talked about how my teaching activity at Europe's top 10 business schools was strengthening the company brand and increasing our ability to attract talent.

Sometimes, none of this will work. In fact, it is easier to get a 10% raise when you join a new company than to get a 5% raise inside your own company, even if you have an excellent record of performance. If you also feel that your work is not appreciated and there is not a good fit, maybe moving on is an option worth considering in order to gain the satisfaction and compensation that you deserve.

10.4 OFFICE POLITICS – NETWORKING

How much time are you investing in networking?

If you are a busy middle manager, most likely not enough.

Like my friend and mentor Alessandro says, 'Work is important. Networking is fundamental.' It is key to invest time in both internal and external networking.

Internal networking involves nurturing relationships over time. It is not about reaching out to your colleagues when you need them but instead involves keeping in touch. This may mean sometimes going for coffee, a drink, or maybe for lunch with your colleagues. Other ways to build your internal network involve looking for opportunities to make a presentation to senior management or to send some regular updates and reports to the leadership team. Something else that you will also find valuable is to join cross-functional initiatives or a company's association that will provide you with the opportunity to meet colleagues across a broader spectrum of people.

Most of the time professionals are not doing enough **external networking**. We know that most of us are unlikely to work with the same company throughout our career. It becomes imperative to keep up the external networking throughout your career.

A good starting point is to join or even create a group of people that work in your same functional area. From my side, I have been the chairman of a Procurement Directors' association for 18 years. It has given me an opportunity to build a close relationship with a wonderful group of professionals that helped me to develop my professional capabilities and also to build a solid network outside.

Other ways that are helpful are to be a speaker at conferences, at alumni events or at other types of occasions. Also, keeping in touch with your former colleagues will enable you to exchange useful information within the industry. For instance, when I left a large pharmaceutical company, one of the things I did, for a period of five years, was to start sending the equivalent of today's newsletter to former colleagues and key suppliers that I appreciated. Every Friday evening, I would send a short message titled 'It is Friday!' that usually involved a joke or something similar. It was mainly a way to stay connected with people with whom I enjoyed working in the past.

Another example was shared by my friend Bhavesh Shah, a former P&G colleague, now a C-level executive. One of the things that he did throughout his career is that whenever he got promoted, changed jobs, or had something important happening in his career, he would send a message to all his previous bosses to inform them about this change and thank them for helping him reach those kinds of levels.

What are your strategies to build your internal and external networks?

10.5 OFFICE POLITICS – UNWRITTEN RULES

Can you mention any unwritten rules at your company?

If you are struggling to find some, then let me share some insights. This is especially important if you are new to the company; you want to ensure you take a moment to understand the unwritten rules that can influence your role.

A good way to start is **to observe, to ask questions and ideally to ask somebody who has been with the company for a long time that can give you insights on how it really works**. Because job titles may not be correlated with influence, the executive assistant of a senior vice-president may be more influential than a director. A chief of staff may be more influential than other people at a higher level of seniority.

The values that are really implemented by the companies may not be the same as were presented on their website or what you are told. In fact, what people mean may be quite different. Let me share an example.

I was working with a large pharmaceutical company, and I was appointed to team up with five colleagues, all from different departments. The team of six had to come up with a different way to approach innovation in the company. The official message was to be bold and to come up with innovative ideas. We worked well together and came up with a number of recommendations. One of us made the presentation at the European team meeting in Helsinki to the top hundred executives in the company to present our recommendations on how to improve our approach to innovation. One of the topics that we had recommended was that innovation starts with the leaders. Unfortunately, this message was perceived by the company's Head of Europe as a personal attack. A couple of months later, the person who made the presentation was made redundant. So, we could be bold and innovative, as long as this would make the big boss look good!

10.6 CHAPTER 10 IN A NUTSHELL

To know your market worth ahead of requesting a raise, you should research both externally (such as talking with people in your network) and internally (such as talking with an internal sponsor).

To make your request for a raise:

- Make a short list of your strongest achievements
- Think carefully about the order of these achievements
- Make a specific request after you have listed your achievements
- Ensure that the number you request is a bit higher than what you really want.

Also, prepare a list of 'yes-able' alternatives in case your request for a raise is denied. They can be in four categories:

- Financial
- Tangible
- Intangible
- Job-related.

Make sure that you make time for internal and external networking throughout your career.

Observe, ask questions and speak with someone who has been in the company for a long time to understand its unwritten rules. This is going to be very beneficial for your career success in future.

CHAPTER 11

INFLUENCING TECHNIQUES

11.1 THE PERSUASIVE POWER OF FRAMING

We start the chapter with the framing effect. The related theory suggests that individuals make decisions based on how an issue is presented, or 'framed'. There are therefore multiple opportunities to use this technique for persuasion and influencing purposes and get another party to pursue a choice that we want them to follow.

Let me start with an application of this technique by a European supermarket chain. Their customers are led to believe that there is a promotion, whereas in fact there is none. What the supermarket does is place a product which *is* actually on sale on one shelf. (In the photo below, the sign in French reads 'Action'.) Then on the next shelf, they have another type of product that is sold at full price, but they put a prominent sign 'Actuel' (meaning 'everyday low prices'), which makes consumers believe that there is a promotion. As you have probably guessed, this application is some sort of manipulation rather than ethical influencing.

At the same supermarket, I noticed a canned tuna supplier that modified the packaging. One part of the packaging was changed to red, with large numbers indicating 4 x 80g. This led people to believe that there was a promotion and that one of the tuna packs was free, while in reality the product was sold at the normal price. The fact that they continued to use this misleading packaging for over two years indicates that it probably helps to increase sales.

Let's look at how professional real estate sellers frame their message in the most effective way. Imagine that you want to buy your dream house. The property is for sale at one million euros, and you offer 950,000 euros. The real estate agent, rather than trying to persuade you to pay the 50,000 euros difference (which sounds like a big number), is more likely to talk about the five percent difference. Or even more persuasively, they may say, 'It is going to make less than 500 euros of difference in your loan.' Of course, you will have to pay these 500 euros more for the next ten years! The technique is to make it appear like the difference is a much smaller amount to persuade the buyer to accept the terms.

Here are some tips to use framing effectively:

1. **Whenever you make a proposal, make sure that you focus on the needs of the other party.** Then, frame proposals and offers in terms of mutual benefits and long-term value. For instance, if you are a job seeker and you are negotiating to get a benefit, do not talk about why this benefit is important to you. Instead, talk about the value for the company when they give you such a benefit.
2. **Aggregate losses and disaggregate gains.** If you have multiple benefits or pieces of good news, present them separately. If you have multiple losses or pieces of bad news, present them all together (see 12.6 for more details).
3. **Leverage relative perception.** By framing smaller purchases against a larger overall amount, people perceive the additional expense as less significant. For instance,

the options added by car sellers do not seem so expensive when viewed in terms of the entire price.

4. **Consider reframing your proposal**. Sometimes your current negotiation positioning is not leading to expected outcomes. If you now developed a better understanding of your counterpart views, you can adjust the framing of your proposal to meet their specific interests and address the reasons for the current impasse.

11.2 APPLYING THE PRIMING EFFECT

In Germany, two psychologists conducted an interesting experiment. In a group, half of the participants were asked, 'Do you believe that the mean temperature in Germany is higher or lower than 20 degrees?'. The other half of the participants were asked, 'Do you believe that the mean temperature in Germany is higher or lower than five degrees?'.

After that, they asked the group to choose words that were randomly available among a set of words. Guess what happened? The people that were given the benchmark of 20 degrees ended up choosing words that were related to summer, like sun or beach. The people that were given the benchmark at five degrees ended up choosing words that were related to winter, like ski or frost.[1]

This experiment is a great introduction to the impact of the priming effect. To share more insights on this topic, here is another experiment that was done in the USA. The researchers asked participants to construct a sentence based on four words. Half the participants were given words that were related to being old, while the other half of the participants were given words that were related to being aggressive. After the experiment, the people who received the words related to being old ended up walking slower as they left the premises, and the people who were given words related to being aggressive ended up demonstrating less respectful behaviour with the people they interacted with after partaking in this experiment.

---

1   R. Dobelli, *The Art of Thinking Clearly* (Harper Paperbacks, 2013).

Priming occurs when an individual's exposure to previous stimuli influences their response to subsequent stimuli, without any conscious awareness of the connection.

Let's try to apply, for instance, the priming effect to negotiation. Imagine we want to create a more collaborative climate into a negotiation. What can we do that is in line with the application of the priming effect?

- We can use collaborative words, such as respectful, fair, and ethics
- We can use 'we' language rather than 'I' language
- We can sit at the corner rather than sitting opposite
- We can use mirroring to connect with the person at the nonverbal level
- We can remind prior positive experiences with the counterpart.

11.3 LEVERAGING SOCIAL PRESSURE

Do you have a tendency to follow what your friends or colleagues are doing?

We all tend to conform to the beliefs and behaviour of the people around us. **This is called peer pressure or social pressure**.

In everyday life, if one applauds at a show, everybody applauds. We follow fashion. We use testimonials (even for this book) to indicate what other respectable people are thinking. Professionals use recommendations in their LinkedIn profiles.

Let me share an example of how I used peer pressure in the corporate world. As I joined the Pharmaceutical giant Novartis, the Over-The-Counter (OTC) division was keener to work with Procurement because they had a need to improve profitability, while the Pharma division enjoyed a stronger financial situation and was less keen to work with Procurement. I therefore started the sourcing activity with the OTC division and delivered very strong results, using the successful examples of the OTC colleagues to get the Pharma division to work with us.

Let's see how to apply social pressure to **encourage a certain behaviour**. In this case, you want to show what other people are doing in the same kind of situation. Let's look, for example, at EasyJet, the European low-cost airline. Whenever you book your flight, you have an indication which tells you there are '106 people that are currently looking at this route'. This is encouraging you to make a purchase to prevent prices going up.

When we look at **discouraging behaviour**, the traditional approach was based on telling people to avoid taking certain actions, while the most effective approach is to indicate the action that goes in the right direction. An effective example is a signpost that I have seen on the Swiss Alps: '98% of the people are not littering'. If most of the people are not littering, then you will not be inclined to do it yourself.

Another key insight about social influence is that we constantly fail to realise just how strongly influenced we are by others. We think that we make our own independent decisions, but often we do not!

11.4 THE WINNER'S CURSE

Imagine in a negotiation you receive a reasonable offer from your counterpart. Should you accept the first offer?

My advice is not to accept the first offer from the counterpart even if it is fair and reasonable. Whenever you accept somebody else's first offer, there is a psychological bias that takes place, which is called the winner's curse. What this means is that the person whose offer was accepted will feel unhappy because they suddenly realise that they have ended up with a raw deal.

Let me explain it with a real-life situation. Imagine you want to buy a BMW. However, your finances are not so great, so you cannot afford a new one. You are looking for second-hand. The kind of BMW you want costs approximately 30,000 euros. After considerable research, you found one at 25,000 euros for sale by a private owner, who lived very far from your location. Still, you go and meet the owner. Maybe you have done a negotiation workshop with me and learnt that you should give yourself some room for negotiation. So, you start the negotiation, and say, 'Listen, it was a difficult year for me. I would love to buy your car; I just cannot afford it. I would love to buy it for 22,000 euros.' The owner of the car looks at his wife and says, 'Okay, let's give it to him at 22,000 euros.' Now you should be ecstatic, right? The market value is 30,000 euros and you ended up getting it at 22,000 euros. It looks like a great deal, but guess what? In your mind, there would be two reflections. The first: 'I should have offered 20,000 euros.' The second: 'What is wrong with the car? If they are prepared to sell it so much below the market value, there must be a catch!'.

Remember the key message: Make sure that you do not let the other party experience the winner's curse. So, **never accept the first offer from your counterpart**.

11.5 OVERCONFIDENCE

I have three lovely daughters, Emma, Sara, and Luisa. The youngest one, Luisa, plays piano pretty well. One of the composers she gets from her piano teacher is Johann Sebastian Bach. I want to test your knowledge about Johann Sebastian Bach. The question is, how many compositions has Bach made? I am not asking for an exact number. Just think of a range, 10 to 50, 100 to 300, 500 to 1,500, or any other range, where you are 98% confident that you are going to get it right.

I hope you wrote down your range, or at least you thought about this range. You should be pretty sure to have the right numbers.

The number of compositions by Sebastian Bach in his lifetime: 1,127. Did you get it right with your range? If not, remember that you were supposed to indicate a range where you were 98% confident. So you probably fell into a psychological trap, **overconfidence bias**.[2] We tend to overestimate our knowledge and ability; it is quite common that this happens through all aspects of life. It may be in investments. It may be in our careers. It may be in projects. It may be in our social life.

For instance, an interesting statistic by Nassim Taleb reveals that 84% of French men consider themselves above-average lovers. Now, of course, without overconfidence, this number should be 50%. Also, all large projects tend to take longer than planned, and to cost more than planned. Well, this is actually due to a combination of two elements. On one

---

2   R. Dobelli, *The Art of Thinking Clearly.*

side, there is overconfidence. And on the other side, people who have a direct interest in the project (consultants, contractors, and suppliers) may have an interest in underestimating the cost.

So be aware that overconfidence is part of your life, particularly if you are a male[3] and if you are an optimistic person.[4] So **when you are confronted with different scenarios, I suggest you focus on the pessimistic one. It is likely to be the most realistic**.

3   D. Moore and P.J. Healy, "The Trouble with Overconfidence," *Psychological Review* 115, no. 2 (2008): 502–517.

4   B. Renerte, J. Hausfeld, and T. Twardawski, "Male and Overconfident Groups Overinvest Due to Inflated Perceived Ability to Beat the Odds," *Frontiers in Behavioural Economics* 2 (2023), https://doi.org/10.3389/frbhe.2023.1111317.

11.6 DEALING WITH CONFIRMATION BIAS

Do you consider yourself to be a rational, logical, and impartial person?

If you replied 'Yes' to this question, maybe you want to think again. Because we may not be as impartial as we think.

We are all impacted by a phenomenon called **confirmation bias**. This means we look for evidence which supports our existing beliefs, while we disregard evidence which is against our existing beliefs. To help you understand more about confirmation bias, here's a classic study from Charles Lord.[5] He shared a qualitative report about death penalties with two groups of people: One group were in favour of capital punishment, while the other group were against it. Imagine what happened. When the report was shared with the group of people who were in favour of capital punishment, they said, 'Look, this report confirms capital punishment works.' Yet when the same report was shared with the group of people who were against capital punishment, they came to the opposite conclusion: 'Absolutely, this study confirms that capital punishment does *not* work.'

Confirmation bias happens all the time in our everyday lives. Perhaps you develop a new strategy, then look for all the evidence showing this strategy is working while disregarding the information which is contrary to your views. Maybe you have an existing view about the impact of Generative AI on humankind, and then you look for all the evidence

---

5   C. G. Lord, L. Ross, and M. Lepper, "Biased Assimilation and Attitude Polarization: The Effects of Prior Theories on Subsequently Considered Evidence," *Journal of Personality and Social Psychology* 37, no. 11 (1979), 2098–2109. https://doi. org/10.1037/0022-3514.37.11.2098

that confirms your existing views. Maybe you look for information online, and you keep looking for those websites that have the same views as yours. As you look for information on YouTube, the algorithm will continue to recommend you videos that confirm the same view.

So, recognising that confirmation bias is part of daily life, what can you do to minimise the effect of confirmation bias?

1. **Write down your beliefs** about some of the important things in your life, such as marriage, career, and education. And **then look for the opposing evidence**.
2. **Reconsider the sources that you use to make important decisions**.
3. **Surround yourself with people with diverse views** and listen to those different views.

How about if you want to help other people resist becoming affected by confirmation bias?

A proven strategy, which was also evidenced by research,[6] is to **encourage people to consider the opposite perspective**. What do we mean? Take the capital punishment study. Suppose it claimed: 'With capital punishment, the number of murders decrease.' Then the groups may have drawn certain conclusions from this data. And then you also ask them: 'But what kind of conclusion would you draw if the data indicated the opposite—that the number of murders *increased*?'.

---

6   S. van Brussel et al., "'Consider the Opposite' – Effects of Elaborative Feedback and Correct Answer Feedback on Reducing Confirmation Bias – A Pre-registered Study," *Contemporary Educational Psychology* 60 (January 2020).

For important decisions, another strategy is to **include the devil's advocate in a team**, which will bring a different perspective to the discussion.

11.7 FLATTERY AND COMPLIMENTS

You may have experienced a salesperson that uses flattery to build a relationship with you. How did you feel about it?

There is a truth that is difficult to admit: We tend to like our flatterers, especially if the flattery is done well. The research on flattery can be summarised with a few words: We are more influenced by flattery than we want to admit!

Personally, I am not a big promoter of flattery. Still, if you want to broaden your toolkit of flattery techniques, here are three techniques that tend to work well:

1. **Pretend you are asking for advice**. Sincerely asking for advice is a powerful influencing technique, because it boosts people's ego and gets them into a problem-solving mode. If we are not really interested in the person's advice, we can use it as a flattery technique.
2. **Arguing before agreeing**. You may pretend to disagree and then agree to their point of view to make them feel like the influencer.
3. **Talk positively about the person with other people**. Of course, you will have to choose the kind of person that is likely to report back your positive comments to the person you are trying to influence.

Instead of using flattery, I would encourage you to **use sincere compliments**. Even with someone whom you do not appreciate much, you can offer a sincere compliment. And if you find something that they do not hear often or something they worked for (rather than a natural quality), it will be even more appreciated. To give a good compliment, make sure to follow these three simple steps:

a) **Make the compliment**
b) **Justify your statement**
c) **Ask a question on the topic**.

Let's say that I want to pay a compliment to Donald Trump. Then I could say something like: 'Donald, I am impressed by your influencing skills. You were able to be re-elected as President of the United States and influence over 77 million Americans to vote for you. When you have to influence people on a one-to-one basis, what technique do you use to understand what will make the other party tick?'.

11.8 CHAPTER 11 IN A NUTSHELL

For better framing of your proposals:

- Focus on the needs of the other party
- Aggregate losses and disaggregate gains
- Leverage relative perception by framing smaller purchases against a larger overall amount
- Consider reframing your proposal.

We can benefit from the priming effect by creating stimuli that will influence the response of our counterpart without their conscious awareness.

Whenever you want to encourage or discourage a certain type of behaviour using social pressure, indicate what other people are doing that goes in the right direction.

Never accept the first offer from your counterpart to prevent them experiencing the winner's curse.

Overconfidence is part of your life, so when you are confronted with different scenarios, focus on the pessimistic one. It is likely to be the most realistic.

To minimise the effect of confirmation bias:

1. Write down your beliefs then look for evidence supporting the opposite conclusion.
2. Reconsider the sources that you generally use to make important decisions.

3. Surround yourself with people with diverse views.

Three techniques for flattery:

- Pretend that you are asking for advice
- Argue before agreeing
- Talk positively about the person with other people.

Even better, replace flattery with a sincere compliment—then justify your statement and ask a well-considered question on the topic.

CHAPTER 12

BROADENING YOUR INFLUENCING SKILLS

12.1 INFLUENCING OTHERS USING LOGIC OR EMOTION

Do you prefer to influence using logic or emotions?

If you went to business school, you are likely to reply: 'It depends.' Let me give you an example so that you can compare the two contexts.

It is 2008, and the US presidential elections are in full heat. The two final candidates are doing a TV debate and get asked the same question by the TV anchor. John McCain speaks about unemployment, and says: 'Four years ago, the unemployment [rate] was 6.1%. Thanks to all the good measures that we put in place, at the beginning of this year the unemployment rate was down to 4.9%. You can count on the Republicans and on me to further reduce unemployment, despite the current economic crisis.'

Then it was the moment for Barack Obama to speak: 'Just 10 days ago, I was chatting with Melinda, a single mother of five children. She had a health problem, and she had to quit her job. When she recovered, she started to look for a job so that she could provide for her children. She sent 1,850 resumes in the last eighteen months, and she could not find a single job. We want a country where everyone that wants to work can work, whether they are old or young, black or white, overqualified or underqualified.'

Which of the two messages did you find more compelling?

Of course, this is an example where you are trying to influence a large group of people. When you want to influence only one person, then you want to consider these three key criteria to determine whether you want to employ logic or emotion.

1. Look at **the personality of the person you want to influence: Is their preference for logic or emotion?**
2. **The relationship that you have with the person**. If you have just met someone, it is better to start with logic. If you are more familiar with the person, then use emotion.
3. Think of **the context, the place, the topic**. For instance, if you want to influence a person that works in engineering, then you are more likely to use logic. If you want to influence someone who works in marketing, you are more likely to use emotion. In general, emotional messages are more effective for immediate decisions as well as individual decisions.

12.2 BUILDING COALITIONS

I was focusing on this topic after I returned from a sunny vacation in Italy. Building coalitions is a topic that had become especially relevant, as the different political parties were discussing forming a viable coalition to form a new government in Italy.

Of course, this topic is just as relevant in a business scenario. If I think about my own experience, I recall a situation when one of my former companies was choosing the location of the new European headquarters. There were several different choices and people had their own preferences and opinions. Senior executives started to look for allies in order to influence the decision-maker to choose their preferred city.

Let me suggest three ways to build a coalition.

First, **persuade the other party that your interests and goals are similar or at least compatible**. In this respect, remember that when building a coalition, it is more effective to remain general in terms of the interests and goals. This is because as you get deeper into the details, you are more likely to end up in a conflicting situation. For instance, when considering the earlier situation of the political parties, it is easier to agree that a common goal is to reduce unemployment. However, it is much more difficult to go into the details on the exact measures that will be used to reduce unemployment. Different parties will prefer their own strategies to reach the same goal.

Second, **indicate to the other party that working together will enhance their ability to reach their goals**. A classic example is the message that unions give to workers: Do not try to be on your own—join a union, and then together we will have more power to put pressure on management so that the interest of the workers will be best defended.

Third, **explain that the benefits of working together are greater than the costs**. In order to convey this message, you typically have two strategies: Either you use incentives, or you use penalties. Let's take a historical example, when the United States used both type of tools to reach their goals. In 2003, they wanted to create a coalition to go to war in Iraq. They used incentives in terms of financial aid or political benefits to incentivise countries to join them. At the same time, they also made it clear that there would be strong disadvantages for those countries that did not choose to join the coalition.

12.3 OFFERING THE RIGHT INCENTIVES TO MOTIVATE

How do you set up the right incentives to motivate and influence people?

Here's an interesting experiment that sheds light on this point. A group of high school students were expected to go door to door to collect money for charity. The group was split into three subgroups. One of these subgroups would receive 10% of all the money that they collected. The second would get 1% of all the money that they collected. The third would receive nothing, with all the money going to charity. Guess which of the three groups collected the most money? It was actually the third group, the one that got no money for themselves. They were doing it because it was the right thing to do. It was linked to their intrinsic motivation.[1]

Let me also share a personal story on the topic. Several years ago, I was launching my first open enrolment negotiation workshop in Zurich, Switzerland and had a limited network there. I therefore offered four senior Procurement executives, who were part of my network, a share of the revenue. (They would get a percentage for each ticket that they would help me sell.) The result: None of the four executives sold a single ticket!

As much as possible, rather than thinking about the carrot or the stick, think about something that will inspire the **intrinsic motivation** in an individual. Social incentives like praise, a gift, and some feedback are usually more effective than monetary incentives, especially with friends.

---

1   R. Dobelli, *The Art of Thinking Clearly* (Harper Paperbacks, 2013).

If you are thinking about increasing intrinsic motivation in your team, remember that **each person has different motivators**. As one of my mentors Andreas says, some of the actions that tend to work with most people include creating opportunities for growth, encouraging autonomy, and providing a sense of purpose.

Another useful tip is to **offer a choice of incentives**. If your team achieves a certain result for a goal, then they have the option of receiving a bonus, a paid vacation to the Maldives, or a few additional days off work. People can then choose from the incentives that they find most appealing.

12.4 HOW TO RECOGNISE A REAL EXPERT

Several years ago, when I still had a corporate job, I attended an advanced negotiation workshop with one of the leading negotiation training firms in the world (one of those large companies with many trainers offering similar content).

It was a three-and-a-half-day workshop. Quite intense. Well structured. We finished late at night. Despite that, there was just one part that surprised me. There was never time for questions. Whenever somebody would ask questions, the trainer would respond, 'Oh, I have no time right now, we have a tight schedule.'

A few years later, I understood why this was happening. I had read a great book by Rolf Dobelli called *The Art of Thinking Clearly*, which I highly recommend. In this book, the author shares the story of Max Planck, who won the Nobel Prize for Physics in 1918. Those were difficult times. The First World War had just ended. Despite that, Max Planck went around Germany to present to fellow professors and colleagues his research on quantum mechanics that enabled him to win the Nobel Prize.

Planck was travelling from one city to another in his chauffeur-driven car, sharing the same presentation. After several days of listening to his presentation, the chauffeur went to him and said, 'I know your presentation by heart. Trust me. I can say it in exactly the same way that you say it. Why not do something different tonight in Munich? I will give the talk, and you can sit in the front row with my chauffeur hat.' Max Planck was open to the idea, although it is unclear if this is true or a legend. So that night in Munich, it was the chauffeur who gave the talk, and indeed he was able to say the same things as Max Planck.

And then the moment arrived for questions from the audience. A physicist asked a fairly difficult question. At that moment, the chauffeur said, 'I am surprised that in a modern and advanced city like Munich, I am asked such simple questions. This is the kind of question that even my chauffeur can answer.' And he pointed to the real Max Planck who was seated in the front row!

Now this story can help us understand the difference between real knowledge and chauffeur knowledge. Real knowledge is based on effort, on studying, on fully understanding the topic. Chauffeur knowledge is about putting on a show, being able to repeat something which has been prepared by somebody else in a way which looks well structured.

In real life, if you have to choose a consultant, a trainer, a journalist that you want to trust, a politician that you want to vote for, how can you distinguish between real knowledge and chauffeur knowledge? The first way is to **ask a lot of questions**, in particular 'Why' questions. The second way is to be aware that **people with real knowledge are also aware of the limits of their knowledge**. If the question is outside of their knowledge, they will not be afraid to respond, 'I don't know.'

12.5 GENDER DIFFERENCES IN INFLUENCING AT BUSINESS MEETINGS

Let me start this paragraph with a disclaimer. When talking about gender differences we should remember that we cannot assume those differences apply to everyone, as there are normal distribution curves of behaviour. We should also recognise that differences in behavioural patterns may also come from other factors, such as status or even the context of the interaction.

Here are some general differences which we may see in the meeting rooms. Our first difference is around communication approaches and goals, because men are more likely to have a meeting for a specific outcome. Besides that, women will also be looking for a possible social connection during the interaction. These subtle differences lead to a different kind of behaviour. **When men are in a meeting, they are more likely to use direct and assertive language.**[2] **They are more likely to make statements rather than ask questions, and more often use 'I-statements'** as opposed to 'we-statements'. They tend to initiate discussions and are less likely to soften their statements with qualifiers.

On the other hand, women tend to use 'we-statements', to take a more collaborative approach in the way they communicate, to ask more questions rather than making statements, and also sometimes use limiting language messages. These include hesitant sentences, like: 'Could it be possible that maybe we look at this.'

---

2   K. Kumari Dash, S. Kumar Dash and S. Satpathy, "A Study on Gender Differences in Workplace Communication across Organizations," *Journal on Interdisciplinary Studies in Humanities* 13, no. 3 (2021), 1–10.

Or maybe minimising words, for example: 'Well, a little bit of that.' The use of a more indirect communication style by women can lead to their contributions being overlooked. This difference is rooted in socialisation patterns, where women are taught to be more communal and cooperative, while men are encouraged to be assertive and dominant.[3]

How this plays out in the meeting may affect the outcome. Let me share with you a real-life story from a female executive friend. She was participating in a decision regarding the launch of our next product, which was a premium tea. As different people start getting together, a male member voiced his opinion: 'I believe we should launch this product in India because it is such a big country.' Another male executive responds: 'Well, no, I believe we should launch it in the UK.' The third male says, 'No, I am convinced that Australia is the right place to launch this product.'

My friend, the female executive, decides to speak up later and asks a question rather than making a statement. 'Should we consider launching it in Japan, which is a country which drinks tea and has a high level of education?'. Her ideas were given little attention, as other colleagues wanted to make a point about their views.

The discussion continues, until 10 minutes later, one of the male executives says, 'I believe we should launch it in Japan.' And then people say, 'Yeah, John, you are right. Let's launch in Japan.' So, John ends up getting the credit for the decision to launch in Japan, while the idea really came from

---

3   Deloitte Report, *Women and Power in Business* 2012, https://www2.deloitte.com/content/dam/Deloitte/global/Documents/About-Deloitte/CE_Women_and_power_report.pdf, accessed 3 April 2025.

the female executive. This reminds us of the importance of receiving validation for our inputs.

Credibility building also differs between genders. Men are generally more comfortable bragging about their expertise and accomplishments, and when they introduce themselves and ideas with this framing, their ideas come across as more credible and influential. By contrast, women have been taught that bragging is 'unladylike' and refrain from sharing their experience, therefore can come across as less credible and influential.[4]

Here's a positive for **female executives**, though: They **tend to be much better at using emotions than men**. Men have more of a tendency to use rational messages while women are better at balancing rational and emotional messages—and we know that it is chiefly emotions that drive us to action.

In addition, to ensure that the ideas and contributions of female participants are properly recognised, you may want to use and encourage a strategy recommended by my friend and colleague Suzanne de Janasz.[5] She talks about **'amplifying' women's contributions**—where colleagues repeat and attribute ideas to the original female speaker, ensuring that women's ideas and contributions are fully recognised and accredited.

---

4   S.C. de Janasz and T. A Scandura, "Ready to Walk," Dialogue Q3 (2022).

5   S.C. de Janasz and V. Mattingly, "Negotiate Like a Woman," Dialogue Q1 (2021).

12.6 HOW TO BREAK GOOD OR BAD NEWS TO YOUR BOSS

Imagine you have to give two pieces of bad news to your boss. Will you give it to her or him in the same meeting or in two separate meetings?

How about if you were to give him or her two pieces of good news? Will you give them in the same meeting or in two separate meetings?

To help you understand the right answer to this question, let us imagine a real-life situation.[6] You are walking down the street, and you find a bill of 10 euros. You pick it up, which makes you happy. The following day you are walking again and find another 10-euro bill. You pick it up, put it in your wallet, and feel happy.

Let's look at another scenario: You walk on the same street and find a bill of 20 euros. You pick it up, and you are happy. Will you be happier finding 10 euros twice or 20 euros once?

Let's now look at it from a different perspective. You look at your wallet and notice that you have lost 10 euros. The following day you check your wallet again, and you have lost another 10 euros. Now in a different situation, you look at your wallet and you have lost 20 euros. Which one of these two situations will make you less unhappy? Losing 10 euros twice or losing 20 euros once?

I'm guessing you all come to the same conclusion. You will be happier to find 10 euros twice, and you will be less unhappy by losing 20 euros once.

---

6   D. Malhotra and M. Bazerman, "Psychological Influence in Negotiation: An Introduction Long Overdue," HBS Working Paper (2008).

So now let's use these examples in delivering good news and bad news, losses and gains.

The key message is to **aggregate losses and disaggregate gains**. The bad news items should be delivered all together in the same meeting, while the good news items should be delivered one by one. This will increase the satisfaction of the other party.

This is one of the applications of the psychological bias called **loss aversion** that describes the tendency of individuals to prefer avoiding losses over acquiring equivalent gains. Another application of loss aversion is formulating your message in a way that focuses on the losses rather than the gains. Otherwise stated, what we tend to say is: 'Let's do this project, because we are going to save a hundred thousand dollars.' A more effective and persuasive approach is instead to say, 'If we do not do this project, we will lose a hundred thousand dollars.'

12.7 HOW YOUR VOICE STRENGTHENS THE CREDIBILITY OF YOUR MESSAGE

For a few years, we have seen a sharp increase in the number of virtual negotiations. As a result, the use of the voice becomes a more prominent element of your communication.

Do you know how to strengthen the credibility of your voice? Let me share with you five effective strategies that I learnt from my friend Dr. Branka Zei.[7]

Use a low pitch. People who speak with a low pitch are perceived as more credible versus those who speak in a high pitch. As reported by *The Times*,[8] CEOs with deeper voices earned, on average, $187,000 more and led companies with $440 million more in assets than those with a pitch of 125Hz. Changing the pitch of your voice requires voice coaching. A simple strategy is, at the beginning of a meeting, to make a conscious effort to lower your pitch for your first message.

Falling intonation. It occurs when your pitch drops at the end of a sentence, which signals confidence and finality. For example, saying 'Let's move forward with this proposal' with a dropping pitch sounds decisive. In contrast, rising intonation means your pitch goes up at the end, which can suggest uncertainty or doubt, as if you're asking a question. In negotiations, this rising tone can be irritating to the other party and reduces your credibility.

Avoid hesitations. All the 'ums' and 'aahs' (disfluencies) that we tend to put into our message decreases the effect

---

7   B. Zei Pollermann, "How to Communicate Charismatically," *IMD Leadership*, February 1, 2024, https://www.imd.org/ibyimd/leadership/how-to-communicate-charismatically.

8   H. Devlin, "Lower the Tone if You Want to Reach the Top of the Corporate Ladder," *The Times*, May 13, 2013.

of your point. Studies[9] show that up to five disfluencies per minute is acceptable. If you have more than five, then it certainly weakens your argument and credibility. Two simple ways to reduce hesitations are to synchronise your hand gestures with the speech rhythm and to use pauses.

Use chunking or make sentences shorter. Cut down messages in short pieces of information. Science[10] shows that our short-term memory can only retain seven units of information, plus or minus two. That means between five and nine pieces of information are absorbed. If our message is too long, our minds and memories cannot retain it, and then it doesn't end up in our long-term memory bank. To ensure that our message is understood and retained by our counterpart, we should make short sentences or chunk down our messages into smaller digestible pieces. To see the chunking technique in action, just watch a video of Barack Obama, a master of chunking down.

Adapt your speech rate. Imagine a situation where you go to see the CEO of your company or a senior vice president. You would naturally experience stress in front of a senior executive, and because of your stress levels you may have a tendency to speak very fast. This does not work to your advantage. To be more effective, adapt your speech rate to that of your counterpart or aim for a speed of about 5 syllables per second.

---

9   N. Zandan, "How to Stop Saying 'Um', 'Ah', and 'You Know'," *Harvard Business Review* (August 2018).

10   "The Magical Number Seven, Plus or Minus Two: Some Limits on Our Capacity for Processing Information", by G.A. Miller, *Psychological Review* 63, no. 2 (1956), 81–97.

12.8 CHAPTER 12 IN A NUTSHELL

The three criteria to determine whether you want to use logic or emotion when influencing a person are:

- The personality of the person you want to influence
- The relationship that you have
- The context, place, and topic.

Three key messages that we want to keep in mind in order to build a coalition effectively are:

- Persuade the other party that your interests and goals are similar, or at least compatible
- Show the other party that the benefits of working together will enhance their ability to reach their goals
- Explain that the benefits of working together are greater than the costs.

Social incentives, such as a praise, a gift or some feedback are usually more effective than monetary incentives, especially with friends. Offering a choice of incentives may also be a powerful approach to motivate people.

To recognise a real expert, ask lots of questions and look at the quality of their answers. Be reassured when, for some topics, they will recognise that they do not know the answer.

When looking at gender differences in influencing, look at your own behaviour and identify which types of things you may want to change in order to be more effective when influencing others during meetings.

When conveying good or bad news to your boss, aggregate losses and disaggregate gains. Group the bad news all together in the same meeting but deliver good news items one by one.

Here are five key vocal techniques to strengthen the credibility of your message:

- Use a low pitch
- Use a falling intonation
- Avoid hesitations
- Use short sentences
- Adapt your speech rate.

CONCLUSION

Thank you for reaching the end of this book! I hope you feel empowered with a broader toolbox that can help you to manage your negotiation more effectively and increase your ability to influence others.

I also hope that this book has helped you to change your perspective on negotiation and influencing from difficult, complicated and competitive processes into powerful communication tools that can help us build better relationships and achieve your goals.

As we reach the close of our book, let me summarise some of the key principles that should stay with you in your efforts to become a better negotiator and influencer:

- **It all starts with a focus on our counterpart**. We will struggle to succeed if we are only focused on our goals, our arguments, our ideas. Our goal should be to understand the interests and priorities of our counterparts. This will then help us encourage them to choose, in their own interest, what we want.
- **Preparation is key to success**. And preparation in writing makes a huge difference. This will help us to elaborate a more comprehensive and strategic approach. Research is a prerequisite for good preparation.
- **Trust-based relationships sharply increase your outcomes**. It starts with making good first impressions, then building rapport and over time establishing

trust-based relationships. We are much more likely to make effective agreements with people we trust.

- **Asking questions and active listening are your biggest allies**. Rather than making our interactions a battle of arguments or using manipulative techniques, we should have a learning attitude when interacting with other people. This will help us to truly understand what is of value for them.

- **Science-based negotiation and influencing techniques help you to maximise your outcomes**. The appropriate use of the tools we have seen in this book will increase our ability to reach agreements and get agreements that are more aligned with our interests and priorities, while building strong relationships with our counterparts.

Another way to deepen your knowledge and understanding of negotiation and influencing is to take advantage of all the resources we identified for you and included in our book's website. For each paragraph, you will find an article and a video to help you go deeper into the topic. You will be able to access these resources on the book website accessible via the QR Code below.

I also want you to remember that knowledge is potential power, while action is power. My advice, now that you have completed this book, is to identify three concrete actions that you want to implement from this book and start moving forward immediately using the '**deliberate practice**' approach. This means paying full attention to specific topics for brief intervals. For example, rather than simply saying 'I want to ask more questions in my negotiations', say 'In my negotiation this afternoon I will ask at least five open-ended questions starting with How or What'. As you consistently and deliberately focus on the development of a few clear competencies, and continue doing this over time, you are much more likely to reap the benefits from this book.

And, as you achieve concrete benefits in your professional and personal life, I hope you will find a moment to drop me an email and let me know how this book has helped you and what can I do to help you develop your skills further. I travel a lot for my training activity, and I would love the opportunity to meet you and your organization to progress the learning journey on this fascinating topic. You will find my contact details in the Author Bio.

Thank you again for your trust in buying and reading this book. I hope you fully leverage the benefits in your professional and personal life of becoming an effective negotiator and influencer.

AUTHOR BIO

Giuseppe Conti is the founder and managing director of CABL (www.cabl.ch), a firm that offers a range of customised training programs in the field of negotiation, influencing, and related areas.

Giuseppe is a seasoned negotiator combining academic content with over 25 years of practitioner experience from his senior Procurement and commercial leadership roles within blue-chip multinationals (Procter & Gamble, Novartis, Firmenich and Merck).

Since 2005, Giuseppe has been an award-winning lecturer, recognised for his lively and interactive training workshops across leading business schools in three continents: Bayes, BSL, Cambridge, EPFL, ESADE, ESSEC, HEC Lausanne, HEC Paris, IESE, IMD, Imperial College, INSEAD, London Business School, Oxford, RSM, SDA Bocconi, University of Geneva, University of St Gallen and VU Amsterdam.

In 2018, he left the corporate world and became a Professor/Visiting Professor in Negotiation & Influencing at a number of leading business schools. In fact, he is the only person who has taught at each of the top 10 business schools in Europe. Giuseppe regularly runs workshops in four continents. To date, corporate leaders from multinational corporations and individuals from over 145 different countries have attended his workshops. His strategic long-term customers include leading multinational corporations such as Novartis, Tetra Pak, Philip Morris, Merck, Schneider Electric, Capgemini, Emerson, and Nestlé.

In 2025, he was ranked #1 worldwide among the Top 30 Global Gurus for Negotiation.

When not in an airplane, Giuseppe resides in Switzerland. His three wonderful daughters are studying in three different countries and in three different languages.

Giuseppe can be reached at giuseppe@cabl.ch

EXTRAS: IF YOU ENJOYED THIS BOOK...

I hope this book has sparked an interest to deepen your understanding about negotiation and influencing.

Here are a few free options to continue the learning journey with me:

- On the following page, you will find the QR code to access the additional learning material for this book (an article and a video for each paragraph of the book)
- Check my website, www.cabl.ch, for a wealth of additional resources
- Register for my negotiation and influencing newsletter (including a new video and article each month): www.cabl.ch/contact-us
- Register for my LinkedIn newsletter, 'Influencing Mastery at Work': https://lnkd.in/efnJBCfv
- Follow me on LinkedIn (I share content daily): www.linkedin.com/in/giuseppeconti
- Follow me on YouTube: https://www.youtube.com/@ContiAdvancedBusinessLearning

We also know that negotiation and influencing are practical skills. A lot of the learning comes from joining a workshop, role-playing with other participants, and gaining valuable feedback on your performance.

If you are interested in organising a workshop for yourself or for your whole team, please write to me at giuseppe@ cabl.ch. I will be happy to take you through our negotiation and influencing solutions, as well as our five-step feedback process.

I look forward to staying in touch and seeing you become a master negotiator and influencer!

ACKNOWLEDGEMENTS

This all started with my late parents, Salvatore and Clara, both teachers, who loved me unconditionally and gave me the willingness to learn and improve myself.

My three older sisters, Cettina, Maria Antonietta and Liliana, also supported me throughout my years with their love and affection.

My passion for negotiation sparked when I joined the P&G Procurement team at their European Headquarters in Brussels. Negotiation was a core area of corporate competence there, where I met many bright minds and wonderful negotiators. In particular, the head of the function, Carlo Soave, became my first role model and inspired me to go deeper into the topic.

Throughout my corporate career of over 25 years, I have had the pleasure to negotiate, influence and be influenced by a variety of colleagues, suppliers and customers. Much of my learning came from observation of successful behaviours and self-reflection after my failures. My mentor Alessandro de Luca placed a special role in increasing my self-awareness, improving my influencing skills and helping me to understand the link between these crucial skills and success in corporate life.

I started my teaching career 20 years ago, in parallel with my corporate roles. Working at the top 10 Business Schools in Europe, I had the opportunity to collaborate with many brilliant professors that helped to me to grow and deepen my knowledge. I would like to mention, in particular, Prof. Owen

Darbishire, Academic Director of the Oxford Programme on Negotiation, with whom I had the pleasure to collaborate for the longest period and build a solid partnership and enduring friendship.

I have gained a lot from the interactions with my students, both at Business Schools and with my corporate customers. Having the opportunity to interact with so many bright people across four continents has challenged my thinking and sharply improved the clarity of my advice.

I would also like to thank all the professors and experienced practitioners who work with me at Conti Advanced Business Learning (see www.cabl.ch/instructors). These impressive people are a constant source of inspiration and growth, as well as a pleasure to work with. I am delighted that I followed the advice of hiring people who are better than me!

A special word goes to my three daughters, Emma, Sara, and Luisa. From the very beginning, they supported me in my teaching activity, from making my videos to doing my accounting, and in all artistic endeavours related to this book (book cover, typesetting, photography, etc.)

I would also like to thank several people who had a direct impact in making this book better:

- Owen Darbishire, Giovanni Aquilanti, Alessandro Comerci and Aahana Sengupta, who read each chapter of my book with great care and provided a wealth of comments and advice
- Alessandro de Luca, Xavier Tallon, Yadvinder Rana, Branka Zei, and Suzanne de Janasz, who provided

feedback on specific sections of the book related to their core expertise.

Thank you also to the photographer Anne Gerzat, who took the front cover photo during a very enjoyable and professional photoshoot.

A special mention to Christian Lukey, who suggested the title of this book to me. Your assistance is highly appreciated.

A warm thank you to the whole team at Passionpreneur Publishing. A special mention to:

- Moustafa Hamwi, who motivated to me to write this book
- Shobha Nihalani, who coached me throughout the writing process
- Timothy Roberts, who took care of editing and proofreading with great accuracy, while also providing valuable advice.

Finally, I would like to thank you, the reader. I am delighted that you chose *Negotiation + Influence = Success*. I hope you enjoy reading it, while gaining a number of ideas that you will be able to put into practice.

WORKS CITED

Ames, D., R. Larrick, and M. Morris. 2012. "Scoring a deal: Valuing outcomes in multi-issue negotiations," *Columbia CaseWorks.* 5 March. Accessed April 3, 2025. https://www.columbia.edu/~ms4992/negotiations/Scoring%20a%20Deal.pdf.

Babcock, L., and L. Laschever. 2003. *Women Don't Ask: Negotiation and the Gender Divide.* Princeton University Press.

Brussel, Suzan van, Miranda Timmermans, Peter Verkoeijen, and Fred Paas. 2020. "'Consider the Opposite' – Effects of Elaborative Feedback and Correct Answer Feedback on Reducing Confirmation Bias – A Pre-registered Study". *Contemporary Educational Psychology.*

Champika, K. October 2024. "The Role of Negotiation Skills in Career Development and Organizational Effectiveness: A Study of Sri Lanka State Universities." *Science and Innovation* 190–4.

Coleman, H. J. J. 2010. *Empowering Yourself: The Organizational Game Revealed.* 2nd ed. Author House.

Covey, S. R. 1989. *The 7 Habits of Highly Effective People.* Free Press.

Curhan, J. R., H. A. Elfenbein, and H. Xu. 2005. "What Do People Value When They Negotiate? Mapping the Domain of Subjective Value in Negotiation." *Journal of Personality and Social Psychology*, 93–512.

Dash, Dr. K. K., Dr. S. K. Dash, and Dr. S. Satpathy. 2021. "A Study on Gender Differences in Workplace

Communication across Organizations." *Journal on Interdisciplinary Studies in Humanities* 1-10.

Deloitte. 2012. *Women and Power in Business.* Accessed April 3, 2025. https://www2.deloitte.com/content/dam/Deloitte/global/Documents/About-Deloitte/CE_Women_and_power_report.pdf.

Devlin, H. 2013. Lower the Tone if You Want to Reach the Top of the Corporate Ladder. *The Times.*

Dobelli, R. 2013. *The Art of Thinking Clearly.* Harper Paperbacks.

Factor, The Culture. n.d. *The Culture Factor.* Country Comparison Tool. Accessed April 3, 2025. https://www.hofstede-insights.com/country-comparison/.

Falcao, H. 2017. *Four Reasons Why Internal Negotiations Are Harder Than External Ones.* July. Accessed April 3, 2025. https://knowledge.insead.edu/leadership-organisations/four-reasons-why-internal-negotiations-are-harder-external-ones.

Fisher, R. and W. Ury. 1981. *Getting to Yes: Negotiating Agreement Without Giving In.* Penguin.

Fisher, R., and D. Shapiro. 2005. *Beyond Reason: Using Emotions as You Negotiate.* Penguin.

Friedman, R., S. T. Tidd, S. C. Currall, and J. Tsai. 2000. "R. A. Friedman et al. What Goes Around Comes Around: The Impact of Personal Conflict Style on Work Conflict and Stress." *The International Journal of Conflict Management* 32–55.

Galinsky, A. D., W. W. Maddux, D. Gilin, and J. B. White. 2008. "Why It Pays to Get Inside the Head of Your Opponent: The Differential Effects of Perspective Taking and Empathy in Negotiations." *Psychological Science* 378–84.

García, A. M., B. Gil-Gómez de Liaño, and D. Pascual-Ezama. 2021. "Gender Differences in Individual Dishonesty Profiles," *Frontiers in Psychology.* 12 December. Accessed April 3, 2025. https://www.frontiersin.org/journals/psychology/articles/10.3389/fpsyg.2021.72 8115/full.

Janasz, S.C. de, and V. Mattingly. 2021. *Negotiate Like a Woman.* Dialogue Q1.

Janasz, S.C. de, and T. A. Scandura. 2022. *Ready to Walk.* Dialogue Q3.

Kahneman, D. 2011. Thinking, Fast and Slow. Farrar, Straus and Giroux.

Kraljič, P. September 1983. Purchasing Must Become Supply Management. *Harvard* Business *Review.*

Leonardelli, G. J., J. Gu, G. McRuer, V. H. Medvec, and A. D Galinsky. May 2005. "G. Leonardelli et al. Multiple Equivalent Simultaneous Offers (MESOs) Reduce the Negotiator Dilemma: How a Choice of First Offers Increases Economic and Relational Outcomes." *Organizational Behavior and Human Decision Processes* 64–83.

Lord, C. G., L. Ross, and M. Lepper. 1979. "Biased Assimilation and Attitude Polarization: The Effects of Prior Theories on Subsequently Considered Evidence." *Journal of Personality and Social Psychology*, https://doi.org/10.1037/0022: 2098–2109.

Maister, D. H., C. H. Green, and R. M. Galford. 2001. *The Trusted Advisor.* Touchstone.

Malhotra, D., and J. A. Davis. 2007. *Five Steps to Better Family Negotiations.* 9 July. Accessed April 3, 2025.

https://www.library.hbs.edu/working-knowledge/
five-steps-to-better-family-negotiations.

Malhotra, D., and M. Bazerman. 2008. *Psychological Influence in Negotiation: An Introduction Long Overdue.* HBS Working Paper.

Malhotra, D., and M. Bazerman. 2007. *Negotiation Genius.* Harvard Business School.

Malhotra, D. 2020. "Process Before Substance." Accessed April 3, 2025. https://www.youtube.com/watch?v=f1OR mtdpJpk. March.

Moore, D., and P. J. Healy. 2008. "The Trouble with Overconfidence." *Psychological Review* 502–517.

Nolan, D. P., and E. T. Anderson. 2015. *Applied Operational Excellence for the Oil, Gas, and Process Industries.* Gulf Professional Publishing.

Pollermann, B. Z. 2024. "How to Communicate Charismatically," IMD Leadership. 1 February. Accessed April 3, 2025. https://www.imd.org/ibyimd/leadership/ how-to-communicate-charismatically/.

Polzer, J. T. 1996. "Intergroup Negotiations." *Journal of Conflict Resolution* 678-98.

Rana, Y. S. 2025. "When AI Joins the Table: How Large Language Models Transform Negotiations." SSRN.

Renerte, B., J. Hausfeld, and T. Twardawski. 2023. "Male and Overconfident Groups Overinvest Due to Inflated Perceived Ability to Beat the Odds." *Frontiers in Behavioural Economics*, Accessed April 3, 2025. https://doi.org/10.3389/ frbhe.2023.1111317.

Research, Accenture. 2015. Accenture Research Finds Listening More Difficult in Today's Digital Workplace. February. Accessed April 3, 2025. https://newsroom.

accenture.com/news/2015/accenture-research-finds-listening-more-difficult-in-todays-digital-workplace.

Stasi, M. J.Q. Di, and M. W. Brooks. September 2024. The Most Effective Negotiation Tactic, According to AI. *Harvard Business Review.*

Thompson, L. 2008. *The Truth About Negotiations.* Pearson Prentice Hall Business.

Zandan, N. August 2018. "How to Stop Saying 'Um', 'Ah', and 'You Know'." *Harvard Business Review.*